OXFORD MONOGRAPHS ON
SOCIAL ANTHROPOLOGY

General Editors

E. E. EVANS-PRITCHARD   B. E. B. FAGG

A. C. MAYER   D. F. POCOCK

Ethology and Society

TOWARDS AN ANTHROPOLOGICAL VIEW

HILARY CALLAN

CLARENDON PRESS · OXFORD

1970

Oxford University Press, Ely House, London W.1

GLASGOW NEW YORK TORONTO MELBOURNE WELLINGTON
CAPE TOWN SALISBURY IBADAN NAIROBI DAR ES SALAAM LUSAKA
ADDIS ABABA BOMBAY CALCUTTA MADRAS KARACHI LAHORE
DACCA KUALA LUMPUR SINGAPORE HONG KONG TOKYO

PRINTED AND BOUND IN ENGLAND BY
HAZELL WATSON AND VINEY LTD
AYLESBURY, BUCKS

To
JOHN AND MARION FLASHMAN

ACKNOWLEDGEMENTS

I WISH to express grateful thanks to the following for advice, encouragement and moral support in the preparation of this work; Dr. M. R. A. Chance, Professor E. E. Evans-Pritchard, Professor Robin Fox, Dr. Derek Freeman, Mr Francis Huxley, Dr. R. G. Lienhardt and Professor N. Tinbergen. Miss Andrena Watts typed the original thesis under far from comfortable conditions. Mr Edwin Ardener was an ideal supervisor and my debt to him is far greater than appears in the occasional acknowledgements I have given in the text. To my husband Ivan my debt is more personal but nonetheless total.

CONTENTS

I

INTRODUCTION

THIS book has been written in an attempt to do some pre-
liminary thinking about the relationship between ethology
and social anthropology; between what Tinbergen[1] has
called 'the biological study of behaviour', and one branch of the
study of human social activity. Many claims are currently being
made about the relevance of animal behaviour to the understanding
of human society; and it seems worth trying to spell out some of
the theoretical questions raised by these claims, even if one cannot
answer any of them. I do not wish to embark on definitions of
'social anthropology' beyond saying that I am thinking primarily
of the 'mainstream' traditions of British social anthropologists. I
propose to follow Tinbergen's general definition of ethology,
although my main concern will be with social behaviour and
organization in animals. The following points, however, are to be
borne in mind.

Firstly, the word 'biological' as used by Tinbergen is a shorthand way of referring to a whole set of premises and assumptions
drawn from traditional and modern evolutionary theory. Specifically, questions about behaviour tend to be asked in terms of its
species-preserving functions, its phylogenetic history and its
ontogenetic development in the organism. The place of evolutionary
theory in anthropology and sociology is a highly complex issue;
and the question naturally arises whether it is a valid procedure
to abstract ethologists' material from the theoretical framework in
which it has been collected, should comparisons of human and
animal social life seem to necessitate this. A misgiving of this kind
may well lie behind Tinbergen's belief[2] that the 'methods' rather
than the 'results' of ethology are of value in the study of human
society. On the other hand, one of the suggestions I shall make is
that the strictly functional approach may not be the only, nor the
most profitable, one for bringing together data from animal and
human social life. Secondly, the term 'ethologist' has tended in the

[1] Tinbergen 1963.   [2] Tinbergen 1968.

past to refer to a fairly small group of scientists, zoologists and naturalists by training, centred mainly in Britain and Europe (notably Holland), who draw their immediate inspiration from the work of Lorenz and Tinbergen, and through them from such pioneers as von Uexküll and Heinroth. It is clear that other material such as the work of the modern primatologists is crucially relevant to any 'biologically oriented' account of human social behaviour; and I shall wish to cite some of these studies while recognizing that they fall outside the Lorenz–Tinbergen tradition, and might well be regarded by the 'classical' ethologists as foreign to their field.

In approaching the relation between ethology and social anthropology, two sets of questions can broadly be asked:

(a) questions about common ground between the two disciplines at the level of data; for example, are there continuities between animal and human social behaviour of such a kind that a common descriptive vocabulary might be appropriate? In the literature, this line of enquiry often links up with questions about the 'biological origin' of this or that institution.[1]

(b) questions about the relevance to one another of ethology and social anthropology as academic disciplines.

These two sets of questions will be expanded and discussed further in Chapter IV. Clearly they are not ultimately independent of each other, and will tend to merge in the treatment of specific topics. For example, in Chapter VIII I set out to discover whether the nature of rank-order systems sheds any light on the position of women in human societies, but this proves impossible without first considering whether the meaning of 'dominance' itself shifts according to the techniques of observation appropriate to different species. Nor are the questions analytically distinct, for before one can decide about 'continuities' one has to be confident of not having begged this very question in the initial allocation of terminologies. In Chapter IV I shall discuss this problem under the label of the 'aha!-reaction'. Nevertheless I wish to separate the two issues initially; because it is possible that answers to the second set of questions may be positive, and answers to the first, negative. Questions of the first type are thus the stronger questions, to the extent that positive answers to them would provide compelling reasons why social anthropologists should be professionally aware

[1] Davis 1962 is a good example.

of what is happening in the behavioural sciences. On the other hand ethology would not be the first discipline with which social anthropology has been claimed to have methodological links.

It is clear that the above outline covers a wide range of material, and in drawing on this material I shall have to be highly selective— perhaps arbitrarily so. This will be particularly true when I come to deal (in Chapters v, vi, vii and viii) with specific topics in ethology, and their relevance to areas of social anthropology. It is my view that the argument for increased contact between the two disciplines will ultimately stand or fall according to the fertility of such contacts when tried out. I wish therefore to stress that this book is intended to outline certain initially discrete areas of potential research, rather than to cover everything that can be said about the relationship between ethology and social anthropology.

THE POSITION OF SOCIAL ANTHROPOLOGY WITH RESPECT TO 'INTERDISCIPLINARY' CONTACTS

A feeling has lately grown within British social anthropology that 'isolationism' imposes a strain on the subject, and that it should be brought to an end. In 1944 Gluckman wrote that 'The status of sociology [of which he took social anthropology to be a branch] largely depends on how far it can claim to be scientific in its procedures and the results it obtains.'[1] He was treating the essential aim of sociology/social anthropology as that of arriving at 'laws' governing closed systems of interrelated social facts. He still, of course, holds this view.[2] But by the 1950's and the closing years of the structural/functionalist heyday, the feeling was often implicit that this brand of isolationism had run its course.[3] As an open complaint, this view was expressed at least as long ago as 1951, when an accusation of isolationism on all fronts underlay much of Murdock's critique of British social anthropology:

The British social anthropologists . . . are as indifferent to the theoretical as to the descriptive writings of their colleagues in other lands. They refer repeatedly to one another on theoretical issues but almost never cite an anthropologist from continental Europe, the United States, or even the British dominions . . .[4]

[1] Gluckman 1944.   [2] See e.g. Devons and Gluckman 1964.
[3] See e.g. Evans-Pritchard 1950.   [4] Murdock 1951.

In a rejoinder published at the same time, Firth is unrepentant about the fact of isolationism, but is ready to agree that it may have outlived its usefulness:

British social anthropology has got its character by isolating its field of enquiry. It has developed at an early stage both a tradition of field research among relatively self-sufficient integral cultures, and a coherent body of theory to explain them. The categories used have been largely conventional. But in ritual, kinship, economics, law, language, politics, British social anthropologists have helped to provide a more precise framework of ideas and substantial propositions.

But at the same time:

What is relevant here is the aim of strengthening linkages between disciplines, not of simply making a case for an old-fashioned—and spurious—unified science of man.[1]

Much has changed since then. It now seems to be true that even those who wish interdisciplinary boundaries to remain more or less intact, recognize that there are neighbouring disciplines in which the social anthropologist cannot hope to be fully competent, but whose content he can no longer afford to ignore.[2] Several recent writers have come out unambiguously against isolationism,[3] and the climate of opinion in Britain is now such that an attempt to establish links of any kind between social anthropology and a neighbouring discipline, can be reasonably sure of a serious hearing.

But how real was this 'isolationism'? Here a useful distinction has been made by Ardener, between the 'pedagogic' and 'epistemological' aspects of an academic discipline. He writes for example: 'Academic disciplines in their pedagogic aspect exhibit

[1] Firth 1951.
[2] See Gluckman (ed.) 1964. Although Devons and Gluckman argue, in their concluding chapter, that when the anthropologist trespasses beyond the limits of his competence he often does, and should, act with conscious naïveté, the whole book testifies to the recognition that in modern social anthropology 'foreign material' impinges on one at every point and must somehow be coped with.
[3] See e.g. Davenport 1963; Firth's proposal (1962) that the ASA should organize a joint meeting with a dozen American social anthropologists 'since the milieux in which the American social anthropologists worked were so much more varied than the milieu [sic] of British social anthropologists . . .'; Freeman 1966; Jarvie 1964. The view is perhaps implicit in Jarvie. But he evidently considers that the dilemma of the structural/functionalist 'cargo cult' can be resolved through 'an interdisciplinary study, and a rebellious one at that' (Preface, p. xx).

modes of recruitment, demographic structures, and ideologies (including mythologies) that are not covered in an epistemological description'.[1] I suspect that the 'isolation' of British social anthropology, of which Murdock and others have complained, was largely confined to its pedagogic aspects so far as these are separable from the epistemological. For example Evans-Pritchard recounts the history of social anthropology, from soon after its origins in British and French social philosophy to the ascendance of the functionalist school, in terms of attempts of varying success to establish links with other disciplines; with evolutionary biology, history and psychology.[2] Ardener records that 'social anthropology was more experimental, even in the 'fifties, than the mainstream literature would suggest. . . .'[3] —and Malinowski himself evidently considered that links were ultimately to be forged, at any rate with 'epistemological' sociology:

Not separable!

> The progress of anthropology towards a really effective analytic science of human society, of human conduct and of human nature, cannot be staved off. To achieve this, however, the science of man has first and foremost to move from so-called savagery into the study of more advanced cultures of the numerically, economically and politically important peoples of the world.[4]

Moreover, Malinowski's interest in the relevance of anthropological data to theories of the unconscious mind, needs no documentation.

If this underlying open-mindedness was obscured during the height of the structural/functionalist influence, the reason may be that a thorough-going functionalism does indeed imply isolationism[5] to the extent that societies are considered to be closed systems, and the fieldwork training of the social anthropologist to provide the equipment necessary and sufficient for arriving at the operating principles of those systems. But this is a paradox; for the adoption of an organic analogy for societies clearly is, epistemologically speaking, an anti-isolationist move.

I feel therefore that it is reasonable to regard British social anthropology as a discipline distinguished not by the exclusive ownership of a range of facts but rather by something else; by a certain traditional stamp, perhaps, a recognizable style in its ways

---

[1] Ardener 1967.   [2] Evans-Pritchard 1950.
[3] Ardener 1965.   [4] Malinowski 1939.
[5] One might almost say that it implies a disciplinary solipsism.

of defining its problems. On this view, the potential validity of interdisciplinary movements *per se* in social anthropology is not in question.

THE NEED FOR SELECTIVITY

A discipline which like social anthropology is inherently plastic, would become vacuous if taken to be infinitely so. The question therefore arises: where are the 'limits of plasticity' of social anthropology? Is there anything to rule out from the start any links between ethology and social anthropology? I suggest that the second question has no answer. This is not the kind of issue that can be settled in advance, still less settled for all time. I have already cited the linkage between anthropology and history, which was tried, rejected, tried again in a new form by Evans-Pritchard, and accepted. A more realistic question would therefore be: how does a 'limit of plasticity' come to be recognized? Part of the answer is clear; by trying out the proposed linkages and working out their consequences at all levels. But this does not tell us much; nor perhaps, can a complete answer be given, since so much depends on the 'pedagogic' element of a discipline, and the often disproportionate influence of particular people at particular times. Thus a 'synchronic' section through social anthropology (perhaps through any academic discipline) might yield a picture which would appear distorted or even arbitrary if one took the time-dimension into account.

Nevertheless I think it is worth looking briefly at one attempted interdisciplinary link which is now generally agreed, at any rate in this country, to have failed. I have in mind the 'culture and personality' school, for which I take Nadel's definition: 'the working assumption that anthropology and the psychology of personality can illuminate one another and can even be combined, to mutual benefit.'[1] I do not wish to deny any possible relevance of a 'psychological dimension' to the study of societies. For one thing,

---

[1] Nadel 1956. It might be fairer to take a less perfunctory summary of the aims of 'culture and personality' such as Benedict's: 'A culture, like an individual, is a more or less consistent pattern of thought and action . . . Taken up by a well-integrated culture, the most ill-assorted acts become characteristic of its peculiar goals, often by the most unlikely metamorphoses. The form that these acts take we can understand only by understanding first the emotional and intellectual mainsprings of that society.' Benedict 1934; Mentor Books edn 1948, p. 42.

this would contradict what I said above about the need for the
frontiers of social anthropology to be perpetually negotiable. But
any successful attempt to link social anthropology with the
psychology of personality will have to be more sophisticated in its
allocation of concepts than was the case in the past.[1] Nor is it
possible here to document very fully the rise and fall of 'culture
and personality' and its reception outside America. I therefore take
Nadel's views as illustrative.

In 1951 Nadel acknowledged the growing popularity of the
'culture and personality' approach; he himself, though trained as a
psychologist, appears to have been sceptical from the start:
'Certainly a prolific literature testifies to the vitality of this combined approach to culture and society, insensible though its exponents may be of methodological scruples.'[2] Yet this school, while
continuing to flourish in America, has virtually disappeared from
view in Britain. Why? In the above remarks of Nadel's the key
words are 'vital' and 'working'. In Nadel's eyes at least, 'culture
and personality' had consciously heuristic aims; it fails on its own
terms, since (again in this country) it is now neither working nor
vital. What is relevant here is whether the school's initial attractions
for the social anthropologist have anything in common with those
of ethology; and whether the reasons for its failure hold a warning
which would also apply to the present programme. We might at
least learn a lesson of caution.

Nadel gives two reasons for the initial attractiveness of the
'culture and personality' link: (a) 'the essential analogy of the two
concepts, culture and personality' and (b) 'the developmental
aspect of the theory of personality.'[3] He argues convincingly that
on both counts the supposed 'natural affinities' between the two
subjects are illusory. Thus on the second point Nadel shows that

[1] See Bruner 1964 for a defence of the 'culture and personality' approach.
One fundamental danger in a 'social psychological' approach to social life, in my
view, is the following. Both the premises and the results of investigations in
social psychology commonly take the form of some variation on the proposition;
individuals tend to choose companions and situations which satisfy their needs.
Now this is unsatisfactory, not for the layman's reason ('they tell you what everybody knows in words nobody can understand') but because it is a disguised
tautology. Much of its predicate is already determined by the logic of the verb
'to choose'. But (and this is where the real questions lie) we don't know *how* much,
until we know more about how situations of choice are set up in the 'real' world,
as opposed to the artificially simple world of the laboratory.
[2] Nadel 1951, p. 289.   [3] ibid. 1956.

the focusing of anthropologists' attention on developmental issues, which promised to yield a useful amalgam of the two approaches, led instead to the hybrid concept of the 'culturally defined personality'. As he says, this concept is unworkable. For a given culture, either there is an infinity of 'cultural personalities' or there is nothing that one could search for in the field, discover and bring back for examination. A broadly comparable danger might arise with respect to ethology. I said above that one must be careful about isolating, for comparative purposes, parts of a coherent and rigidly controlled intellectual system such as unifies modern 'mainstream' ethology. Ethology and social anthropology differ in a number of ways, not least in the nature of the generalizations appropriate to each. The problems of verifiability in the social and biological sciences are crucially relevant here. If, failing to recognize this, one were to use ethological vocabulary uncritically in order to 'explain' human social facts, the result might well be a set of bastard concepts and postulates which have no place in either field. An example of this kind of mistake is Morris's talk of 'pair-bonding' in human beings as if this were equivalent to a social institution.[1] Here of course the mistake arises from lack of sociological, not biological, sophistication. Similarly, one frequently hears ethologists speak of 'dominance-subordinance' in human relations, and it is seldom made clear exactly what this is supposed to mean.

To return to Nadel's first point; he argues that 'culture and personality' fails because of the ultimate barrenness of the culture-personality analogy. It may be true, he says, that '. . . in describing a culture we describe on a collective scale the kind of readiness-cum-behaviour which indicates the personality', but 'so far the framework of personality psychology offers to the anthropologist nothing in the way of really new information, only a new method of describing it.' Here we have an even closer parallel to the present case. For much of the attractiveness of ethology, *prima facie*, for the social anthropologist lies in apparent analogies between the social processes of animals and men. A common vocabulary often seems to be broadly applicable—consider for example the terms 'threat', 'appeasement', 'ritualization'. At the moment the question is thoroughly open whether we can ultimately get beyond a mere listing of such supposed analogies, and perhaps a use of ethological

[1] Morris 1967. See also Chapters IV and X, *intro.*

terms in firm quotation marks to describe bits of human social action. But even to speak of 'analogies' may be falsely encouraging. Nadel might have added that much of the 'analogy' between culture and personality may derive from descriptions which presuppose the very parallels they are called on to exhibit. I have said already (p. 2) that there is an ever-present danger of this kind of circularity in comparing the 'sociology' of animal and human groups. This point will arise again more than once in the chapters to follow.

In spite of all this, I would suggest that the barrenness of the culture–personality link was visible only in retrospect. This then becomes a further argument for not prejudging the outcome for ethology and social anthropology.

These, then, seem to be the initial and obvious problems in a search for links between ethology and social anthropology. I have emphasized my view that, given the climate of thinking in British social anthropology today, there is little or no doubt about the respectability of interdisciplinary studies as such (though I note the dissenting view of Devons and Gluckman on this point). I have touched on the problem of what constitutes the success or failure of an interdisciplinary study; and have suggested that while it may be impossible to identify in advance criteria of success, an examination of Nadel's views on 'culture and personality' has revealed at least two retrospective criteria of failure. I acknowledge that these hold a general and a specific warning for the present programme.

The only possible conclusion is that the ultimate evaluation of this programme must be an operational one; and this justifies undertaking the inquiry whatever its outcome. For if, at worst, the ethology–anthropology link is as barren as the culture–personality parallel, it like the latter will be even more visibly so in retrospect; and something will have been learned. In Chapters III and x, I shall show that the possible relevance of ethology to social anthropology is at least a promising enough question to have attracted some interest in the recent literature.

II

EARLY LITERATURE

I SHOULD like at this point to digress briefly from the theory of the two disciplines under discussion to their origins and history. This will involve, throughout most of this chapter, a consideration of the relations between biological and social science in general, rather than between ethology and social anthropology in particular. It is sometimes said that biology and sociology exerted little or no influence on one another after (roughly) the beginning of the twentieth century. Halsey, for example, has suggested that 'It may be that the hostility of sociologists to biological theories of society was intrinsically necessary to the establishment of sociology as a discipline in the following half-century [i.e. after Galton's death in 1911].'[1] There are a number of reasons why this should have been the case, and the point will be raised again briefly in Chapter III. But it is worth looking at a few of the ideas which, in a diffuse way, influenced the thought of men whom modern ethologists and social anthropologists look back to as their founding fathers and grandfathers; at a time before either discipline 'gelled' into its present theoretical mould. Without laying great stress on the matter, I take this to have happened (very roughly) for ethology with Lloyd Morgan's Canon of 1894 insisting on a totally objective approach to the study of animal behaviour; and for sociology with the founding of the *Anneé Sociologique* school.

No full coverage of this topic is remotely possible in a work of this kind. The undertaking would be both too large and too small. It is unquestionable that there were certain ideas dominating (for example) nineteenth century thought; this is amply documented in almost any introductory textbook of social anthropology.[2] On the other hand, to trace and document in detail the progress of a single relevant theme, such as the idea of evolution, as it passes from hand to hand throughout the nineteenth century, would be an

[1] Halsey 1967.
[2] Notably by R. G. Lienhardt in Chapter I of his *Social Anthropology* (1964).

intolerably tedious project. It would also be a misguided one, since one would be starting off from a false position; the picture, that is, of sociology and biology in the nineteenth century self-consciously joining forces, only to be cast asunder because of the very naïveté and enthusiasm with which they had seized on each other's models. This picture might be partly true; for example, it might help to account for 'Social Darwinism' and its consequences. I shall argue below that the consequences of 'Social Darwinism' are probably more important than the doctrine itself was at the time. But it would be more accurate to view the apparently constant spilling over of ideas between sociology and biology in the nineteenth century as a simple consequence of the fact that present-day disciplinary boundaries had not yet been drawn; hence scholars' fields of interest tended naturally to cut across the divisions of a later academic structure. It has been said of ethology that:

During its earliest years, ethology was not a discipline that seemed to require any particular kind of professional training or acumen. Anyone with an eye for the antics of animals and the ability—once more generously fostered than today—to describe these literately (and, prefer-ably, humorously) could style himself a contributor to this field.[1]

The same could be said, *mutatis mutandis*, of social anthropology in its early years. In taking this line, I am following Burrow's general approach to Victorian social theory: 'It is here that modern specialization, the acceptance of lines of division between anthropology and history and philosophy, however necessary today, does a disservice to the study of a past to which such rigidity has no application.'[2]

PRE-NINETEENTH-CENTURY THOUGHT

It is doubtful whether there is much point in pursuing disci-plines such as ethology and social anthropology back to their remotest origins—which in any case bear little relation to the subjects as currently understood and practised. The history of European ideas about animal behaviour before Darwin has been discussed by Warden[3], who places the origins of ethology firmly in the 'close connections between animal lore and religio-magical

---

[1] Klopfer & Hailman 1967, p. 26.   [2] Burrow 1966, p. 17.
[3] Warden 1927. See also Bierens de Haan 1948.

rites ... during the thousands of years that elapsed before the birth of science.'

The main point to be noted about this pre-Darwinian (or more accurately, pre-evolutionary) era, is that an ideologically based dichotomy between the essential natures of human and animal life appears very early in European thought.

> By the time of Galen ... a fairly definite concept of instinct appears to have emerged. The foundation had thus been laid for a sharp dichotomy between man and the brute creation—the one possessing reason and guided by experience, the other endowed with an instinctive life in which individual experience plays at most a subordinate role. This distinction was further developed ... in connection with the doctrines of the church, and became the ruling conception in the discussions of the mental life of animals during the middle ages.[1]

Cartesian philosophy both exhibits the crux of the problem and solves it unequivocally. To quote Warden once more:

> The extreme mind-body dualism of Descartes ... amounted to a flat rejection of the nutritive soul of Aristotle in favour of a purely mechanical explanation of bodily processes ... the animal must either be granted an immortal soul or be classed along with man's body as a purely physical machine. Descartes chose the latter alternative and held that the animal is a natural machine (la bête machine).[2]

This state of affairs was bound to persist, roughly speaking, as long as the mainstream of philosophy (in this country at least) was dominated by the idea of rationality as the defining characteristic of man.[3] It is significant here because such a climate of thinking would tend to play down observation of those areas in which animal and human behaviour resemble one another; although oddly enough it does not seem to have discouraged comparisons between animals and men at a level of social organization. But there is not a great deal to say about the earliest fore-runners of anthropology

---

[1] ibid.

[2] ibid. 1927. See also Bierens de Haan 1948, and Lowenstein 1964. Lowenstein distinguishes between 'mechanisms' and 'machines' of which only the former concept, he says, covers animals and men's bodies on a Cartesian view. He advocates a return to 'the simplicity of a monistic world-picture' but at the same time gives credit to Descartes for laying 'the foundation for the development of mechanistic physiology'.

[3] But see Locke's (1690) discussion of identity, which he illustrates with a charming story about a rational parrot. *Essay concerning human understanding* (Everyman edn) vol. 1, 278–80.

and ethology, considered in relation to one another. The remote origins of social anthropology range from travellers' tales to a general philosophy of man and society; those of ethology, from traditional animal lore to the growth of a systematic biology typified in the work of Linnaeus and of Cuvier.

DARWIN AND WALLACE

The work of these writers provides an obvious landmark for anyone studying the development of evolutionary thought in the nineteenth century as it affected both the biological and the social science of the future. But although it would be hard to exaggerate Darwin's importance, in particular, in the history of science, it would be easy to over-stress his position as a focus for the convergence of biology and sociology in his day. This follows from what I said above about the relative lack of disciplinary demarcations at that time. But in addition, Burrow rightly criticizes 'the over-use of Darwin in accounting for the rapid development of anthropology in the third quarter of the last century.'[1] As he says, even 'Social Darwinism' was not simply 'a by-product of the *Origin of Species*.'[2] Thus:

The history of Darwin's influence on social theory belongs, except in the case of the theory of natural selection, to the history of the diffusion of ideas rather than of their development. In this context, Darwin was undoubtedly important, but it is a type of importance impossible to estimate at all precisely. He was certainly not the father of evolutionary anthropology, but possibly he was its wealthy uncle[3]

It is in the idea of evolution itself, with all its implications, that the beginnings of ethology do seem to merge with those of social anthropology in the nineteenth century. Among these implications are: the interest in finding original forms from which evolutionary development proceeds; the concern for setting up accurate and systematic classifications; and the idea of a biological continuum linking man with all other forms of life. I therefore propose to concentrate on these themes rather than on Darwin, Wallace or the other 'figures' of the period, outstanding though these men unquestionably were.

But first the well-known point must be made that even the

[1] Burrow 1966, pp. 19–20.   [2] ibid., p. 21.   [3] ibid., p. 114.

specifically biological theory of evolution owes much to the body of philosophical, including sociological, thinking which preceded it. It has been pointed out (by Halsey and Carr-Saunders for example[1]) that both Darwin and Wallace hit on the essentials of the evolutionary process after a chance reading of Malthus' work on population. Wallace speaks for both:

... both Darwin and myself, at the critical period when our minds were fully stored with a considerable body of preserved information and reflection bearing upon the problem to be solved, had our attention directed to the system of positive checks as expounded by Malthus in his *Principle of Population*. It is an unimportant detail that Darwin read this book two years after his return from his voyage, while I read it before I went abroad and it was a sudden recollection of its teachings that caused the solution to flash upon me.[2]

THE IDEA OF EVOLUTION

I argued earlier in this chapter that it would be both misleading and tedious to try to document every point at which evolutionary biologists and sociologists influenced one another. It tends to be assumed that all significant contact between Darwinian biology and contemporary social theory took the form of 'Social Darwinism' —i.e. an uncritical adoption of Darwinian principles by pragmatic sociologists in order to justify reactionary political doctrines. But Lowie, writing as a historian of anthropology, implicitly locates an 'evolutionary mentality' prior to both evolutionary biology and evolutionary sociology.[3] If it can be said that there was an overall cognitive problem facing the mid-Victorian thinkers, then it can be argued that the 'evolutionary mentality' was an overall answer to it. The point is well made by Burrow:

The specific attraction of evolutionary social theories was that they offered a way of reformulating the essential unity of mankind, while avoiding the current objections to the older (e.g. Utilitarian) theories of a human nature everywhere essentially the same. Mankind was one not because it was everywhere the same, but because the differences represented different stages in the same process. And by agreeing to call the process progress one could convert the social theory into a moral and political one. . . .[4]

[1] Halsey 1967. Carr-Saunders 1922, p. 34.
[2] Wallace 1915. Cited by Carr-Saunders 1922, p. 35.
[3] Lowie 1937, esp. p. 23.　　　　　　[4] Burrow 1966, p. 98.

Theories of social evolution had provided for the Victorians an intellectual resting-place, a point of repose at which the tension between the need for certainty and the need to accommodate more diverse social facts, and more subtle ways of interpreting them, than the traditional certainties allowed for reached a kind of temporary equilibrium.[1]

Crude 'Social Darwinism', on this view, belongs on the theoretical sidelines in relation to the total philosophy of the period; although it is certainly one possible consequence of the latter. But the influence of 'Social Darwinism' on the subsequent development of social anthropology does seem to have been disproportionately great.[2] In view of this influence, it might be an advantage to know more precisely how much 'Social Darwinism' owed to Darwin—but even here the task would be a hard one. Here is a 'conventional' view of the influence of the natural-selection theory on contemporary social science. The authors admit that such influence was based on a misreading of Darwin, yet;

. . . as Darwin's theories of natural selection and evolution gained ascendancy, Darwinism was increasingly interpreted as providing a natural sanction for current social and economic doctrine. 'Survival of the fittest' became an excuse for the maintenance of ruthless social practices. This in turn led to an increasing distortion of the picture of the animal kingdom. Inter- and intra-specific relations of non-human animals were then seen mirroring human competitive relations in all their ugly details. The romantic notions of an earlier breed of naturalists and philosophers (e.g. Goethe, Rousseau) were rejected in toto. Far from being a peaceful kingdom, animate nature was brutal, selfish, bloodthirsty. For man to be less, to give expression to altruistic impulses, was for him to deny his true nature; this was apparently a common nineteenth-century view.[3]

Given this picture, one can hardly blame a later generation of idealistic sociologists for rejecting the evolutionary model of society. But Darwin himself seems to have ridiculed the idea that the theory of evolution had direct political consequences. His son recounts, for example, that an address given by Virchow in 1877 linked the Descent Theory with Socialism. The resulting brouhaha culminated in the *Kreuz Zeitung* throwing '"all the blame" of the

---

[1] ibid. 1966, p. 263.   [2] See e.g. Halsey 1967.
[3] Klopfer & Hailman 1967, p. 138.

treasonable attempts of the democrats Hödel and Nobiling ...
directly on the theory of descent ...' Darwin père commented
mildly: 'What a foolish idea seems to prevail in Germany on the
connection between socialism and evolution through natural
selection!'[1] It certainly seems a little puzzling that the Descent
Theory should have been linked with Socialism rather than its
opposite. Evidently the distinction is being made between a
society based on inherited wealth and privilege and one based
on unrestricted competition—what we should call *laisser-faire*
capitalism.

Herbert Spencer was certainly a 'Social Darwinist' by 1850—
nine years, that is, before the publication of *Origin of Species*—if by
'Social Darwinism' is meant the attitude shown in Spencer's own
imaginary review of his *Social Statics*. He quotes himself as maintaining that in man as among animals 'the destroying agencies at
work, continually weed out the sickly, the malformed and the least
fleet or powerful,' whereby 'all vitiation of the race through the
multiplication of its inferior samples is prevented'; and as drawing
the explicit corollary that the state ought to aid, not hinder, this
'beneficent, though severe, discipline.'[2]

We can thus conclude that this manifestation of evolutionary
theory as a social and political ideology owes little to Darwin himself; because such views were in the air long before 1859 and also
because Darwin seems to have had no interest in political applica-
tions of his theory. It remains to be decided whether 'Social
Darwinism' was in fact the most important result, at the time, of the
impact of evolutionary thinking on social theory. Here I suspect
that the account by Klopfer and Hailman, quoted above, is more
vivid than accurate. Burrow takes a more sober view, placing
'Social Darwinism' in a context of wider issues. 'Social Darwinism',
he says, is simply the crudest of a number of ways of 'deriving an
ethical and political theory from evolutionary sociology'—by
deducing it, that is, 'from the supposed mechanism of the evolutionary process.' No particular stress was laid on the theory of
natural selection by Maine, Tylor nor McLennan, and even
Spencer 'used it only as a garnish for a theory he had already
developed.'[3] This may be compared with Ginsberg's denial that
either Tylor or Spencer was guilty of arguing from the biological

---

[1] Darwin 1887, vol. 2, pp. 236–7.   [2] Spencer 1904, vol. 1, p. 363.
[3] Burrow 1966, pp. 267, 115.

theory of descent to the existence of 'stages' through which all societies must pass in the same order.[1]

Spencer's career, incidentally, illustrates the difficulty of trying to trace the exact lines of influence and emulation among the evolutionary thinkers of this period. Despite his claim that his 'Development Hypothesis' was formulated independently of the more or less concurrent developments in biology (and he seems to have been somewhat sensitive on this point[2]) and despite the fact that he long held a Lamarckian view of biological change,[3] he appears to have been quite rapidly absorbed, both personally and intellectually, into the orbit of the evolutionary biologists. Thus Darwin writes to Spencer in November 1858; 'Your remarks on the general argument of the so-called development theory seem to me admirable. I am at present preparing an Abstract of a larger work on the changes of species; but I treat the subject simply as a naturalist, and not from a general point of view, otherwise, in my opinion, your argument could not have been improved on, and might have been quoted by me with great advantage.' (Darwin 1887, vol. 1, p. 141.) Again, we find in Chapter III of *The Origin of Species*: 'I have called this principle, by which each slight variation, if useful, is preserved, by the term natural selection, in order to mark its relation to man's power of selection. But the expression often used by Mr. Herbert Spencer, of the Survival of the Fittest, is more accurate, and is sometimes more convenient.'[4] Spencer and T. H. Huxley met in 1852 or thereabouts and became close friends. Huxley admired Spencer as the only non-biologist he knew in the period 1851-8 'whose knowledge and capacity compelled respect, and who was, at the same time, a thorough-going evolutionist.'[5]

These associations have certainly dominated later anthropologists' assessments of Spencer.[6]

THE SEARCH FOR ORIGINS

How things have come to be what they are—how they have naturally grown into their present forms—seems to have become a question which in every case presented itself; with the result that some fragment of the general theory of evolution was more or less definitely sketched out.[7]

[1] Ginsberg 1961, pp. 198-9.   [2] See e.g. Spencer 1904, vol. 1, p. 387.
[3] See Klopfer & Hailman 1967, p. 5.
[4] Cited in Kroeber & Waterman 1931, p. 17.   [5] Huxley, 1887.
[6] See e.g. Evans-Pritchard 1963.   [7] Spencer 1904, vol. 1, p. 442.

This theme, of course, recurs in nineteenth-century thinking over a wide range of subjects; and is inseparable from the concern with catalogues and classifications, equally characteristic of the period. This dual concern has a direct analogue in the preoccupations of modern ethology (see Chapter IV, p. 41). As it applied to nineteenth century social anthropology it needs no documentation; it can probably be linked with the virtual domination of much scientific thought by geology, paleontology and related disciplines.

Geology, paleontology, evolutionary biology, comparative philology and prehistoric archaeology—all, be it noted, with the exception of philology, related by their common dependence on geology—were all concerned with the reconstruction of states no longer directly observable, by means of the classification into stages and the postulation of laws or sequences of development. It is understandable, therefore, that the intellectual life of the period exhibits many cross-currents, some surprising, and some, probably untraceable.[1]

There is evidence too that ethology, when it first began to be conceived as a separate discipline, was given a place in this overall programme: 'The ultimate aim of comparative psychology, according to Romanes, is classification . . . a classification of psychological traits that revealed phyletic affinities and allowed one to trace the course of mental evolution.'[2] From the same stable, clearly, is Dr. James Hunt's view that it was 'for the student of [anthropology] to assign to each race the position it shall hold . . .'.[3]

THE IDEA OF A 'CONTINUUM'

Darwin's *Descent of Man* is largely devoted to the demonstration that something already implied in the idea of evolution—the biological relatedness of all species to one another—firmly attaches the human species to the rest of the animate world. This involves him in a discussion of behavioural, as well as morphological, affinities between man and the brute creation. His constant use of anthropological source material—McLennan, Tylor, Spencer, Lubbock[4]—reflects an assumption that 'low savages' in their

[1] Burrow 1966, pp. 108–9. See also Lowie 1937, p. 23.
[2] Klopfer & Hailman 1967, p. 12.
[3] Cited in Lienhardt 1964, p. 8.
[4] See e.g. Darwin 1871 (2nd edn.), pp. 65, 67, 85, 92, 94, 95 and many others.

mental life are closer to the animal than is any civilized race. But it is also true that the idea of social evolution requires, in a sense, an opposite emphasis. Evolutionary anthropology insists that all human societies (all, at least, which show themselves fit to survive) are subject in common to certain laws of development destined to bring them at last to the condition of Europe and America of the 1870's. Hence the races of man are in all essentials more like each other than like any animal. This may or may not have appeared as an awkwardness in the developing of evolutionary ideas. But if it did, the concept of 'mental evolution' (taken up by Darwin himself in *The Descent of Man* and by numerous later writers) promised a resolution. Given a general climate of evolutionary thought, 'mental evolution' offers a common starting-point for the comparative study of both animal species and human societies. This would be true whether 'social evolution' were thought of as continuous or (as Tylor seems to have felt[1]) merely analogous in some sense, with the corresponding process in biology. Indeed the ideas of 'mental' and 'social' evolution would merge easily with one another, at a time before psychological reductionism was frowned on in the best sociological circles.

But for Darwin and his immediate followers, the problem was almost as much ideological as empirical. Lienhardt[2] suggests that prejudice influenced Darwin's account of the Fuegians and even his selection of ethnographic material on them; and in reading *The Descent of Man* one is constantly being struck by his keen involvement—startling in so sober a writer—in defending the instinctual systems of animals at the expense of the supposedly depraved habits of some savages. He remarks, half-jokingly: 'Judging by the hideous ornaments, and the equally hideous music admired by most savages, it might be argued that their aesthetic faculty was not so highly developed as in certain animals, for instance, as in birds.'[3] But the following is more serious because it implies a real moral condemnation;

As Sir John Lubbock has well observed, 'It is not too much to say that the horrible dread of unknown evil hangs like a thick cloud over savage life, and embitters every pleasure.' These miserable and indirect consequences of our highest faculties may be compared with the incidental and occasional mistakes of the instincts of the lower animals. . . . This

[1] See Marett 1936, p. 19.   [2] Lienhardt 1964, pp. 12–14.
[3] Darwin 1871, p. 93.

is almost the blackest fact in natural history, unless indeed ... [animals']
instinct or reason leads them to expel an injured companion, lest beasts
of prey, including man, should be tempted to follow the troop. In this
case their conduct is not much worse than that of the North American
Indians, who leave their feeble comrades to perish on the plains; or
the Fijians, who, when their parents get old, or fall ill, bury them alive.[1]

Yet here, too, it would be hard to decide to what extent Darwin is
imprisoned in the inherent bias of his ethnographic sources.

This chapter has been necessarily both digressive and derivative,
owing to the nature of the material and the impossibility of attempting a full and critical account. The historical connections between
social anthropology and ethology turn out admittedly to be tenuous;
arising partly from a few personalities like Spencer and Lubbock
(whose work spans the beginnings of both disciplines) and partly
from a climate of evolutionary thinking in the nineteenth century
which naturally affected both subjects in a broadly similar way.

The question of 'Social Darwinism' is, in the present context,
something of a red herring. But even a very brief discussion of it
served to illustrate the difficulty of trying to trace specific lines of
influence—and also emphasized the ideological issues which seem
at that period to have dominated all discussion of Darwinian
evolution as it applied to man. This is familiar ground.

But a further complicating factor is the methodology with which
these early thinkers approached their material. The need (whose
origins were themselves complex) to show that human and animal
life were continuous in important ways, generated the concept of
'mental evolution' which in turn stimulated a crop of anecdotal
writings about the mental life of the higher animals. Warden, in
writing of the 'anecdotal school' or 'the anthropomorphists' (among
whom he includes Darwin, Lubbock, Brehm and Romanes as
'conservative representatives') possibly exaggerates the unity of
this group. But there is no doubt that the contrary reaction of
Loeb and Lloyd Morgan, leading to the latter's famous Canon
mentioned above, was a self-consciously methodological move.[2]
It is interesting to note too that Darwin, when he is not citing

[1] ibid., pp. 96, 102.
[2] Comparable, perhaps, to Durkheim's of 1895. I have in mind the discussion
which begins: 'The first and most fundamental rule is: consider social facts as
things.' Durkheim 1895 (Paperback edn), p. 14.

ethnographic sources, argues in the main from anecdotes about the mental powers of animals but feels quite free to speculate (as in Chapter 3 of *The Descent of Man*) about the thought processes of savages—much as an earlier generation of social philosophers had done.

The conclusion of this chapter is really that there is plenty of evidence of connections, especially in the context of evolutionary theory, between early biology and early sociology. To document all these connections, and the reasons for their having come virtually to an end in the early 1900's, would be beyond the present scope. Modern ethology and social anthropology have their roots, of course, in this same early biological and social theory. But specific linkages between the comparative study of human social institutions and the behaviour of animals, are not so easy to discover. I have suggested that the connections are to be found more indirectly in the thought of the period, which was wrestling with the ideas of 'mental evolution' and of the continuities between men and animals arising from their common participation in evolutionary processes. A final quotation from Warden's article will illustrate the total merging of ideological and methodological with epistemological questions in later Victorian thinking about the area of overlap between animal and human nature.

... the anecdotal school, which flourished for about 3 decades following the announcement of Darwin's theory, set themselves the task of showing that mental continuity was an indubitable fact. Their problem narrowed down pretty much to that of proving that the higher animals possessed a rudimentary reason from which the intellectual life of man might conceivably have evolved. For traditional theology and science had placed the real gap between man and the higher animals. This group was willing enough to concede mental continuity if only man were left out of the scheme. In fact, the old doctrine of 'instincts' was a tacit acknowledgement of such continuity below man. That much of man's behaviour was activated by instinct ... could also be conceded, so long as the primacy of man as the sole reasoning animal was not questioned. But the doctrine of evolution did question this, and therefore forced the issue. And the need of the hour was for evidence of reasoning and other characteristically human mental life in the higher animals.[1]

[1] Warden 1927.

III

RECENT LITERATURE

I PROPOSE to say very little about the relations between biological and social science between (roughly) the beginning of this century, and the very recent past. Halsey[1] speaks of 'relations of suspicion and hostility' between biology and sociology which soon replaced the Darwin/Spencer rapport; and which have largely persisted until the present day. The reader is referred to his paper for a discussion of some of the reasons why this happened. He lays considerable stress on the rejection by a generation of egalitarian sociologists of 'Social Darwinism and the politically reactionary doctrines which have been associated with "the biological approach" to the study of man.' A further point is that since ethology began to claim the status of a scientific discipline, many of its practitioners have concerned themselves with the exhaustive study of 'instincts' and instinctive behaviour. This (and the climate of psychological thinking current at the time) ensured that virtually any human comparisons would concern behaviour at a purely individual level. Now there was no lack of sociologists, such as Hobson and Ginsberg[2], interested in human instincts. But their concern seems inevitably to have been to discover what human actions could be explained by 'instinct' or 'human nature', *in contrast* to those which had to be explained sociologically. In effect, the instinct/culture, biology/society, and individual fact/social fact dichotomies were thoroughly merged, and only the latter half of each was seen as the concern of the sociologist. The question seems never to have been raised whether descriptions which are genuinely sociological can also belong in the biological sphere and apply to both human and animal cases—although many of the most fundamental concepts of ethology, such as the rank-order or the pair-bond, imply a supra-individual level of analysis.[3] Fletcher, him-

[1] Halsey 1967.
[2] See Fletcher 1957.
[3] The converse suggestion, of course, is that there is no automatic opposition between individual facts and cultural statements. It is time this one was sorted out, too.

self concerned with the question of human instincts, sums up the position almost unwittingly:

Ginsberg (like Hobhouse) also emphasizes the importance of the Social Tradition as a determinant of human behaviour, and this serves to drive home the point that thinkers who supported the theory of instincts by no means held that this provided a complete explanation of human experience and behaviour . . . not a single writer who supported the early theory of instincts denied the importance of the social environment as a determining influence upon human behaviour. On the contrary, all admitted it.

It is to be noted that to accept the instinctive basis of human nature is *not* to deny the facts of cultural diversity.[1]

Finally, in accounting for the disillusionment of the twentieth century sociologists with biological models, one may cite the petering-out of the 'evolutionary mentality' and the general weakening of people's faith in laws of universal progress. Ginsberg[2] gives a number of reasons for this loss of belief, perhaps the most important being the rise of Freud and the increased recognition that much human action is irrationally determined. It is not absolutely clear how far the 'law' of inevitable progress had depended on a premiss that man would gain more and more rational control over his destiny; but it seems that at any rate for the eighteenth century thinkers, especially Condorcet, rationality was built-in and crucial.[3] Then again, the belief in progress failed because the social taxonomies, which were intended to parallel those of biology and to document the fact of development, failed to materialize.[4] This continues to be a difficulty for any neo-evolutionary model of society which tries to compare existing human societies and their transformations on the basis of a simple analogy with evolution in the biological sphere.

But here is a paradox; the early alliance between biological and sociological thinking produced, it seems, unwarranted promises of continuing social progress; and was rejected partly for this reason. Yet one result of admitting, now, the relevance of modern ethology to the study of societies, might be that we are forced to recognize that social 'progress', far from being guaranteed, has limits set to it—limits following *a fortiori* from limits set by biological factors

---

[1] Fletcher 1957, pp. 67, 46.
[2] Ginsberg 1961, chapter 1, esp. pp. 8–9.
[3] ibid., pp. 12–13.   [4] ibid., p. 31.

on social change. The question how far this compels a deterministic view of society, I prefer to leave alone.

We turn now to the principal theme of this chapter: recent literature dealing with the present and future relations between ethology and social anthropology. The aim is to arrive at a general view of the present position in the two disciplines *vis-à-vis* one another; and this in turn will serve as a background to my own suggestions. It must once again be borne in mind that I am using the label 'ethology' to cover a wider range of data than might be acceptable to many 'classical' ethologists, although the discussion will, I hope, contain nothing to contravene Tinbergen's definition of the subject which I quoted in Chapter 1. Indeed to define ethology as 'the biological study of behaviour' is itself an implicit act of bridge-building, since it invites investigation whether it is possible to study human behaviour 'biologically'.

THE ANTHROPOLOGISTS

Recently (in relation to the time of writing, 1968) there have been indications of a growing interest among certain social anthropologists in the findings and formulations of ethology. Several writers—notably Tiger and Fox[1] and Freeman[2]—have suggested that the methods and data of ethology may be both useful and necessary for an adequate understanding of human societies. It is too early yet to say whether this interest will gain sufficient ground to become a 'movement' in social anthropology.[3]

Both Tiger and Fox, and Freeman, claim to be dissatisfied with the traditional 'working assumptions' of social anthropology, and dissatisfied in particular with its self-imposed disciplinary boundaries. Each of these writers feels, for different reasons, that social anthropology with its traditional assumptions has worked itself into a rut of some kind, because the question has been begged: 'what, if anything, is biologically given?', in human social behaviour (Tiger and Fox), or because of the dogmas, rooted in Durkheim and upheld by modern writers such as Beattie, that 'social facts are

---

[1] Tiger and Fox 1966.   [2] Freeman 1966.

[3] It is worth mentioning, however, that the 1968 examination papers for the Oxford Diploma in Social Anthropology contain, for the first time, several questions with a directly ethological slant. In addition, irrespective of the anthropological scene, ethological thinking is in the air at the moment (see Chapter x).

(a) of a different order from any other kind of fact, and (b) explicable only in terms of other social facts' (Freeman). They agree that now is the time to resolve this 'conceptual tread-mill' by a fresh examination of the biological sciences, because it is now that the latters' findings have become abundant and sophisticated enough to permit comparison with those of social anthropology. They go further and insist that such comparisons press on the anthropologist whether he likes it or not; 'The data force us into a position of readiness' (Tiger and Fox); '. . . anthropologists cannot afford to be professionally oblivious of physical and biological facts (as opposed to their social images) "for they are concerned with the social impact of physical facts as they are, and not merely as they appear."' Freeman further invokes '. . . the spirit and sense of one of the most significant developments of modern science'— i.e. the trend towards the integration of disciplines.

Tiger and Fox seem to feel most strongly the need to introduce into social anthropology a set of concepts capable of giving it both a greater internal unity and a continuity with the biological sciences. They lay stress on traditional evolutionary theory because 'Darwinian phylogenetic analysis' is 'an intellectual system capable of achieving this integration'. Thus, on their view, '. . . the study of human social behaviour becomes a subfield of the comparative zoology of animal behaviour and is broadly subject to the same kind of analysis and interpretation.' Freeman, on the other hand, gives the impression of being more concerned with bridge-building for its own sake:

. . . the time has come when new tasks need to be tackled. Prominent among these is the task of relating the findings of social anthropology to those of the fast developing behavioural sciences . . . Scientific progress is going to necessitate the gradual abandonment of hard and fast disciplinary boundaries and the increasing devotion of attention to the investigation of basic and pervasive processes which determine events at interrelated levels of behavioural integration.

The essential point of Freeman's argument is that there is no reason—logical or heuristic—for treating the social and the biological sciences as being in principle separate fields. This lies behind his rejection of the standpoints of Devons and Gluckman (see Chapter 1) and Beattie; and through them of Durkheim, on this question.

I do not wish to endorse everything which is said in these articles, although obviously I am in broad agreement with the authors about the need to see how far we can get on a 'biological' view of human social life. It seems to me that Tiger and Fox in particular exhibit the pitfalls of too straightforward a treatment of these problems; and I have certain criticisms to make of their rather sweeping approach.

Tiger and Fox adopt a straightforwardly evolutionary approach to the study of behaviour (although it is only fair to acknowledge that they have misgivings about the term 'Darwinism'). They want to rearrange and if necessary re-assemble anthropological material so as to fit it into categories about which functional and evolutionary questions can be asked. Thus they want more stress (and here I agree with them) on the constants of social life, and they seem to take it that the variables will emerge in some one-to-one relation with local selection pressures. This last assumption is more difficult to uphold. But principally, it seems to me that their view of 'Darwinism' is seriously inaccurate. They say that the key concepts of Darwinism are survival, adaptation and selection pressure, and imply that these can be imported more or less wholesale into the study of human social life. They leave out something essential to the system: random variability within a certain range, with respect to a given characteristic.[1] Given this variability, selection pressures—whether environmental or intra-specific—ensure a preponderance of survivals in a certain direction, the range of variation in turn is shifted in that direction; and so we get the 'directionality' of evolution, on a Darwinian model. Tiger and Fox want to investigate the 'limits of plasticity' of cultures, and this might correspond to the Darwinist's 'range of possible variations'. But they want to do it by 'detailed comparative analysis of cultural variability'—surely begging their own question and leaving us with the proposition that societies can vary inside the limits within which they do vary. I imagine that few Darwinists would accept

---

[1] Huxley (1955) explains the point as follows: 'The mechanism of transmissible variation . . . in all organisms, is twofold —mutation or change in intrinsic properties of parts of the gene-complex and recombination of already existing mutants to produce new variants.' Cf Lorenz 1966, *On Aggression*, p. 146: 'One of the great constructors of the change in species, selection, always requires some fortuitously arising material to work on, and its blind but busy colleague, mutation, provides the material.' For a discussion of the rôle of random processes and events in evolution, see Simpson 1958.

this as defining the *possibilities* 'given' at any time, since it ignores the negative, maladaptive end of the range entirely; and it is clearly no basis for establishing the 'direction' of social evolution, which is what the authors are after. 'Direction' from what starting-points? The programme advocated by Tiger and Fox provides no possibility of an answer—even were it worth arguing about whether the history of evolution, in respect of societies, is a history of successes or of failures. We must also bear in mind the above-mentioned difficulty over evolutionary transformation, the demonstration of which depends on the establishment of accurate taxonomies. This is a problem for Tiger and Fox to the extent that they recommend an evolutionary approach to cultural variation. In the main, however, they are concerned to discover the common parameters of all human social life, as a basis for evolutionary statements about *Homo sapiens.*

Tiger and Fox are quite right when they say that 'one way of looking at human social action is as the result of a prolonged process of natural selection'—certainly it is worth experimenting with this approach. My quarrel is with their use, on a Darwinian model, of cultural variability as the index of the 'limits of plasticity' of societies. I should like to see an alternative view developed: namely, that the first thing we need is a vocabulary sufficiently 'pure' to define the logical possibilities inherent in the notion of social organization as such. Then we can go on to ask in what ways the specific characteristics of man impose restrictions on this range of possibilities; and so gain a new perspective on cultural differences. To put the thing at its most bombastic, I feel that one outcome of an ethology/anthropology collaboration, if it works, should be a new kind of answer to questions to do with 'what is man?'

It would be wrong, however, to be over-critical of Tiger and Fox. It is probably a fact of the sociology of academic disciplines that when suggestions are made for the first time they are apt to be made in an exaggerated and sweeping manner. Tiger and Fox as well as Freeman are at any rate committed to the view that contact of some kind between social anthropology and the biological sciences is necessary and possible. This is a stand, if a somewhat uninformative one; Tiger and Fox are of course more explicit in their emphasis on traditional evolutionary theory. It is worth noting that none of these authors explores the possibility of studying the relation between animal and human social life while leaving open the question of their phylogeny; although Freeman makes a start when he writes of 'basic and pervasive processes which determine events at interrelated levels of behavioural integration.' This fact stems, of course, from the traditional evolutionary approach which is by definition a phylogenetic one. And, of course, the evolutionary history of universals of human behaviour is interesting in its own right. But I suspect that the strictly phylogenetic approach to this topic is not the only possible one. The fact of evolutionary convergence may give us a model for speculating about possible variations on biologically 'given' structural themes. This strategy in turn would largely absolve the anthropologist from a rigid adherence to Darwinian selection in the narrowest sense, while not robbing him of the advantages of the 'biologically minded' approach. This idea of comparable structures (in some sense) as well as functional continuities and evolutionary homologies as a basis for ethological comparisons in social anthropology, is taken up repeatedly in the chapters to follow. In Chapter IV I return to the biological concepts of convergence, analogy and homology, and the complex interplay between them.

Another feature of the Tiger/Fox/Freeman approach is the assumption, contained in both articles, that the links between ethology and social anthropology are to be found via the study of genetically transmitted impulses and patterns in human behaviour at the level of individuals. This assumption is well within the 'human-instincts' tradition of thought which I mentioned earlier in this chapter. Tiger and Fox hold that: '. . . the emerging interdisciplinary approach proceeds not from the analysis of social systems *per se*, but from the selection and transmission of genetically programmed behavioural as well as anatomical systems, which are the unitary bases of human social organization.' Freeman's position is less clear, for he claims that 'social facts' in Durkheim's sense are not the only 'social facts' relevant to the understanding of human society. There are in both human and animal cases, he says, other 'social facts' or '. . . phylogenetically based forms of social response, which decisively determine, in varying ways, the course of social behaviour and the nature of social relationships.' From this one might think that Freeman was attempting to bring together ethological and anthropological thinking via a minimally defined 'sociology' common to both. But as an example of a 'social fact' in animals, he gives not a dominance hierarchy nor a pair-bond but the displacement grass-pulling of herring-gulls. By 'social facts' in animals he evidently means 'instinctive' social releasers, and he compares these not with anything which an anthropologist would take as a 'social fact' but with the (probably innately determined) gestures and intention movements which signal human motivational states. For Freeman, too, the chief relevance of ethology to social anthropology lies in the fact that through the mechanisms of behavioural inheritance, individuals are endowed with certain discoverable patterns of motivation and action, whose nature must be understood before social institutions can be properly analysed. 'The scientific study of cultural adaptations necessarily involves the study of man's impulsive nature which is integral to adaptation.'

All this is very true. But it is puzzling to find in the recent anthropological literature a relative lack of interest in developing a 'sociological' approach to animal studies, whereby at a supra-individual level of analysis genuine 'social facts' might be discovered in animals, and these might be compared with aspects of human social organization. Apart from the anthropologists who are interested in the evolution of human institutions from primate social systems,[1] Mary Douglas is the only social anthropologist I have come across who seems to envisage direct comparisons between aspects of 'social structure' in animal and in human cases. Her work on 'sociological' mechanisms of population control is discussed in Chapter v. One may also mention Halsey's remark, in connection with the same topic of population control; '... sociological factors have to be recognized as by no means confined to human populations.'[2]

THE ETHOLOGISTS

At the moment, ethologists are showing interest in the study of human beings in a number of discrete ways, not all of which are directly relevant to human sociology. Ethological techniques have

[1] See e.g. Fox 1967. There are also, of course, anthropologists interested in the relationships between animal signalling systems and human language considered as aspects of social organization. But I regard this as a specialized field in its own right and beyond my competence to evaluate.
[2] Halsey 1967.

been used with some success in observing the social behaviour of small children[1] and schizophrenic patients.[2] Here the emphasis is very much on 'behaviour' (rather than any developed idea of 'social organization') as the focus of any link between animal and human data. This echoes the predominant bias of the anthropologists, which I discussed above. It is true in general that ethologists locate the significance of their work for the human field within a psychology, rather than a sociology, of human affairs.[3] This may reflect a double misapprehension, for as I suggest elsewhere (p. 127) many social psychologists tend rather insensitively to appropriate the whole of social life under the head of 'social behaviour'—a term which rules out any but the behaviourist's approach. It is possible that this fact has led some ethologists misguidedly to relate their findings to human psychology, when they 'mean' human sociology.

Harlow is one writer (he probably would not call himself an ethologist) who, while concentrating on 'behaviour', gives a clear and interesting indication of the point at which his findings might be relevant to human societal patterns. He demonstrates that there are clear-cut differences between the social responses of male and female infant macaques; and goes on:

I am convinced that these data have almost total generality to man . . . These secondary sex-behaviour differences probably exist throughout the primate order, and moreover, they are innately determined biological differences regardless of any cultural overlap. Because of their nature they tend automatically to produce sexual segregation during middle and later childhood, but fortunately this separation is neither complete nor permanent. Behavioural differences may very well make

---

[1] Blurton Jones 1967; cf. also Gray 1958.

[2] Grant, 1965. Ardener (personal communication) believes that animal and human communication differ importantly in that the former lacks the meta-level of operation. It may be that small children and schizophrenic patients both look as if they ought to be studied ethologically because this same meta-communicative level is largely absent—or at least relatively un-emphasized—in both. Nursery-school children of 3–5 years, though undeniably verbal, are possibly not yet efficiently meta-verbal. And having a schizophrenic breakdown may regularly involve losing one's grasp of the more demanding components of the human communicative equipment—including, perhaps, many of its meta-communicative components. But for an opposing view of the possibilities of animal communication see Altmann (1962), who argues that meta-communication is exhibited by rhesus macaques 'in distinguishing between play and non-play, in communicating status, and in transmitting a message to a particular individual.'

[3] See e.g. Tinbergen 1957.

it easy through cultural means to impose a sexual latency period in the human being from childhood to puberty. We emphasize the fact that the latency period is not a biological stage in which primary sex behaviour is suppressed, but a cultural stage built upon secondary behaviour differences.[1]

The recent and continuing field-work boom in primatology has stimulated a second area of ethological interest in human affairs. This time direct comparisons are made between animal and human material at a sociological level, for the ambition is to show how certain features of human society (such as incest taboos) could have evolved from the basic social organization and living conditions of early primates and pre-hominids. Kortlandt and Kooij[2] and Reynolds[3] have recently been at work in this area; and their interest, as I said above, is shared by some social anthropologists—notably by Robin Fox.

Both primate sociology, and the ethology of children and mental patients, are comparatively new fields of research. More long-standing is the habit, shared by very many ethologists, of mentioning 'in passing' and in a vague manner that whatever they are talking about is significant in human as well as animal contexts, at either the individual or the social level. An early example may be taken from Katz:

The far-reaching parallels, existing as they do between social groups of higher animals and human beings, have led to the conclusion that many sociological phenomena, which so far have been considered as typical for human communities, are yet to be judged as characteristic of all socially living animals, including man.[4]

Numerous other examples could be cited; in fact almost every well-known ethologist has somewhere or other come out with a similar pronouncement. Often, of course, these pronouncements are true as far as they go; but sometimes they betray the fact that

[1] Harlow 1962.   [2] e.g. Kortlandt & Kooij 1963.
[3] Reynolds 1966 and subsequent correspondence in *Man*. In the course of this correspondence, Reynolds claims that he is reacting against the over-use by Durkheimian social anthropologists of 'social factors in the explanation of social phenomena.' (*Man*, NS2, 302–3). He seems to be blurring the individual/social and biological/cultural dichotomies in a familiar way (see above, p. 22) for there is no reason why a biological determinant of cultural forms should not also be a social one.
[4] Katz 1937, pp. 198–9.

their authors are sociologically ill-informed. This is true of Wynne-Edwards' arguments about population control in primitive societies, as I shall argue in Chapter v. Hediger's information about primitive life seems to have been drawn from Darwin or *his* ethnographic sources:

The creativeness of the energy released in man makes its appearance in the beginnings and development of culture, which has reached different levels in different races. Among primitive natives we find . . . that they have broken out of the animal's escape circle, but are none the less at the mercy of the still irresistible urge to escape from the countless demons that infest their subjective world. Thus major importance must be attached to release from the escape circle.[1]

This occupational habit among ethologists, of throwing out vague but hopeful remarks about the significance of their findings in the human context, shades into the current phenomenon which I label 'ethologism' and discuss in Chapter x. It is only fair to add that some of the ethologists' suggestions, though general, are both informed and informative. Kalmus for example shows some originality in arguing that some of the 'concepts and approaches' of human sociology could usefully be adopted by anyone studying animal social organization.[2] Calhoun—again in an 'aside'—echoes much of what I said in Chapter i and will develop in Chapter iv:

. . . Research on the behaviour of animals may provide insight into the human condition with regard to either its evolution or its present circumstances. The utility of such insights depends upon there being a relationship between the present human condition and its antecedents in simpler forms of mammals, or on the fact that comparable processes characterise both man and lower forms.[3]

It is a reasonable guess that most modern ethologists would not want to rule out in principle any contact between their discipline and the social sciences, even though they have not so far pursued such contacts with any degree of sophistication. Freeman cites the views of Huxley and Tinbergen, for example, on the trend towards the integration of disciplines.[4] Many ethologists are in addition keenly interested in investigating the relationships between their

[1] Hediger 1955, pp. 49–50.   [2] Kalmus 1965.
[3] Calhoun 1966.   [4] Freeman 1966.

own findings and those of other disciplines—notably of neuro-physiology[1] and psychoanalysis.[2]

THE PRESENT POSITION

There undoubtedly exists in this country a growing interest in exploring the areas of overlap between the biological and social sciences in general—encompassing, as well as social anthropology and ethology, human biology, genetics, demography, and other related disciplines. In the case of social anthropology and ethology, this growth of interest has so far been a little one-sided. I suggest that the reason for this is to be found in a real difference between the two disciplines. European ethology has always been (*pace* Devons and Gluckman) a more genuinely closed system of thought than has British social anthropology. Its methodology has been more unanimously accepted as adequate to its subject matter; because one of its founding premisses has been that certain recognizable patterns of animal behaviour form coherent systems describable in terms of a limited set of Darwinian principles. Ethologists have been and are interested in relating their findings to those of neighbouring disciplines, but this activity has never been felt to necessitate any re-examination of the fundamental assumptions of ethology. Of course the history of social anthropology is full of attempts to establish a similar autonomy for this discipline, but never, it will be conceded, has this been achieved with such lasting conviction as in the case of ethology. There are questions, it seems, which are chronically open for social anthropology. In Chapter 1 I hinted that the autonomy of British social anthropology was traditionally more 'pedagogic' than 'epistemological'—social anthropology is, by definition almost, a discipline blurred at its theoretical edges. It is therefore hardly surprising that social anthropologists should be more prone than ethologists to have uneasy suspicions that the findings of neighbouring disciplines may be crucially relevant, at all levels, to their own.

What, then, has come of this growth of interest, such as it is?

[1] See e.g. Hess 1962, esp. p. 159; Brown & Hunsperger 1963.
[2] Cf. Lorenz 1964, p. 121; '. . . drives are endogenously generated and . . . energy is needed to repress them. The chief and, in my opinion, most important agreement between psychoanalysis and ethology concerns this dynamic side of instinct physiology.'

The answer must be that not much has yet materialized in the way of actual productive co-operation between ethologists and social anthropologists. The literature I have discussed so far, impressive though much of it is, really counts as kite-flying. Both social anthropologists and ethologists have so far underestimated the theoretical gulf which lies between their two disciplines. On the one hand, I have stated where I think Tiger and Fox go wrong with an over-simple view of the applicability of traditional Darwinian explanations to events in human societies. On the other side, one easily gains the impression that the elegant parsimony of ethological theory tempts its exponents into airy pronouncements on the nature of human social relationships. Lorenz, for example, is particularly prone to do this kind of thing, both in *On Aggression* and elsewhere. I shall suggest in Chapter IV, that misapprehensions about the straightforward applicability of ethological findings to human social contexts must be partly put down to a rather uncritical allocation of terminology on the part of etholo-gists themselves; together with a certain lack of scruple in the use of quotation marks.

Two recently published symposia represent honest attempts to get to grips with the problem of establishing a meaningful dialogue between ethologists and social anthropologists. Yet even in these symposia, real communication between the two camps is surpris-ingly limited. In *The Natural History of Aggression*,[1] mutual understanding between the sociological and biological participants is impeded by an uneasy split between the 'aggression-is-an-instinct' tradition and the old 'frustration-aggression' formula rooted in a mechanistic social psychology. Hence the discussions of the papers, as published, are disappointingly fragmented. In *Ritualization of Behaviour in Animals and Man*[2] the ethologists and social anthropologists did not even manage to agree on a common definition of 'ritualization' (although there was apparently some feeling that this was not a bad thing). The papers by Leach[3] and Francis Huxley[4], and Turner's *Anthropological Epilogue*[5] (it is probably no accident that they are all anthropologists) represent the most interesting attempts to assimilate both ethological and anthropological points of view in this symposium. Their contribu-

[1] Carthy & Ebling (eds.) 1964.   [2] Huxley (ed.) 1966.
[3] Leach 1966, ibid.   [4] Huxley, F. J. 1966, ibid.
[5] Turner 1966, ibid.

tions contain a number of good ideas which ought to be developed further.

So the present state of relations between ethology and social anthropology in this country is that there is much goodwill and many good intentions, particularly on the anthropological side, but rather little in the way of real communication and integration of approaches. It seems to me that if progress is to be made, it must begin with more joint undertakings and reorganizations in the 'pedagogic' sphere, although Halsey has aptly remarked that 'conferences and symposia, admirable though they are, are not enough. We must reconstruct academic boundaries to achieve our purpose.'[1]

[1] Halsey 1967.

IV

THE LEVELS OF CONTACT[1]

IN Chapters II and III, I discussed from a 'pedagogic' point of view certain linkages between social anthropology and ethology: the ideas which the early forerunners of the two disciplines shared with one another and the state of current thinking (so far as it exists) on the possibilities of greater contact between the disciplines now and in the future. At this point I should like to set these considerations aside, and enquire as openmindedly as possible what kinds of contact could in fact occur between social anthropology and ethology, and in what ways each discipline can be considered 'relevant' to the other. This chapter, in other words, represents a shift from a broadly 'pedagogic' to a broadly 'epistemological' standpoint. This is not to assume that the 'pedagogic' element can be dismissed in any simple manner. For one way of phrasing the sort of speculation that may emerge from an enquiry like this is to wonder whether 'doing anthropology' and 'doing ethology' turn out to be rather similar kinds of activity involving comparable problems and comparable academic anxieties.

In Chapter I, I made a distinction between two groups of questions which could be asked about the relation between social anthropology and ethology. I wish now to expand these to at least four levels[2] at which relations might be discovered between the disciplines, and which form a framework for the following discussion. The 'levels' I propose to discuss can be roughly termed those of procedure, of data, of theory and finally a pragmatic or applied 'level'.

THE LEVEL OF PROCEDURE

This is the level at which we may consider analogies between the positions of ethologists and social anthropologists in relation to

[1] The idea of 'levels' of contact between one discipline and another is taken directly from E.W. Ardener's Oxford lectures on linguistics and social anthropology.

[2] With, however, some misgivings about the word 'level'; since firstly the 'levels' are interlinked and not discrete, and secondly they do not form a homologous series of any kind.

their objects of study on the one hand, and their academic colleagues or more general audience on the other. The first point to
be noted is that in both disciplines the object of study, characteristically, is not rigidly laid down, although the type of thinking
applied to it may be. Indeed, in both cases one may well be tempted
to define the boundaries of the discipline either historically or
operationally. For example, Tinbergen, as we have seen, favours a
definition of ethology in terms of 'biological thinking' applied to
behaviour; but he also quotes a remark made by Lorenz at a
conference, that ethology is 'the branch of research started by
Oskar Heinroth.'[1] The analogy is partly of breadth of range in the
data; and is probably connected with the historical fact, mentioned in Chapter II, that both ethology and social anthropology in
their embryonic phases were hunting-grounds for the non-
specialist. Both disciplines are concerned with a wide variety of
observations which overlap those of neighbouring fields—psychology, physiology, genetics and so forth in the one case and law,
demography, economics etc. in the other. In each case the discipline is distinguished from these neighbours more by its characteristic manner of approaching and assimilating the data than by any
exclusiveness of the latter. Hinde writes of ethology that:

... the approach is essentially a broad one, and many of these 'ethological'
studies could equally be classified as psychological, zoological, taxonomic,
ecological, physiological, endocrinological, pharmacological, genetic or
even botanic. The specific characteristics of the work thus lie not in its
scope but in matters of attitude and emphasis.[2]

Although, for both disciplines, the definition of the 'object of
study' is a relatively loose one, this definition has in both cases
tended to include a proviso about 'the natural situation' in some
sense. For ethology, this is explicit; and is often given as a defining
characteristic marking off ethology from (in particular) the
experimental psychology of behaviour. Even where animals have
to be studied in a captive laboratory environment ethology
emphasizes total sequences of behaviour in full relation to their
'natural' setting. This is quite foreign to the approach of (say) the
classical learning theorist, who '... in an attempt to reduce
variability, often not only purposely restricts the behaviour of the

[1] Tinbergen 1963.   [2] Hinde 1959.

animal in which he is interested, but also limits sharply the aspects which he is willing to record.'[1]

It would be unsophisticated, of course, to apply this kind of thinking directly to modern human societies, however 'primitive'—although I have been asked by an ethologist whether social anthropologists go into the field 'to study human beings in their natural habitat.' But there is a similar emphasis, for anthropology, on social structures as 'totalities' composed of interrelating institutions. Partly for this reason, anthropologists have traditionally placed great value on observations of 'preliterate' societies before they came under the influence of Western civilization in its various manifestations; and have tried to relate social institutions to the functioning of a society in its traditional, 'uncontaminated' form.[2] Thus we have two dichotomies which may be comparably significant in social anthropology and ethology respectively: traditional/Westernized and wild/domesticated, where the concept of domestication is taken widely enough to include all radical human interference in the life of a species.

But if these oppositions are analogues in the two disciplines, they are, for analogous reasons, becoming less and less useful. Without doubt, the anthropologists have been the first to recognize this. It is not now seriously questioned that social anthropology needs to concern itself with 'urban' and 'literate' communities, and (whether or not one accepts 'social change' as a separate field of study) with the interactions of 'Western' and 'traditional' elements in societies. But the wild/domesticated opposition (particularly in the broad sense I have adopted) seems destined to go the same way. Klopfer and Hailman cite Herre's work on

a number of changes in brain morphology that are common to domestic forms of a wide range of species, from dogs to ducks. Apparently, some as yet undefined conditions of domestication affect all domestic stock, irrespective of the particular kinds of characters for which the stock in question is being selected.[3]

Domestication itself takes many generations to bring about such fundamental changes; yet remembering how rapidly human activities are altering the living and breeding conditions of animal species in even the remotest habitats, it may soon be quite

[1] ibid.
[2] The 'organic analogy' and its implications are relevant here.
[3] Klopfer & Hailman 1967, p. 186. See also Hale 1962.

valueless to contrast the 'natural' with any other kind of situation. The emphasis on totality will presumably remain, as it does (as far as possible) in social anthropology. But one may well ask whether the present tense, in which the typical ethogram is written, may come to sound as disembodied as the 'ethnographic present' frequently does in anthropology today.[1]

In this connection it is worth retelling a tale apparently hoary among ethologists. An experiment of Tinbergen's[2] revealed phylogenetically adapted responses to flying predators of a particular shape, in turkeys, pheasants and greylag geese. Hirsch, Lindley and Tolman repeated the experiment in 1955 using white leghorn chickens; and found no such specific responses. They concluded: 'The Tinbergen hypothesis ... was tested on the white leghorn chicken, and found untenable under strict laboratory conditions.'[3]

Lorenz comments:

This statement is exactly as meaningful as if somebody were to have demonstrated the presence of melanin in the hair of wild common hamsters and if somebody else were to have written: 'The Somebody theory that there are melanins in the fur of wild hamsters was tested on white laboratory rats and found untenable under strict laboratory conditions.'[4]

The above points about the way ethology and social anthropology define their objects of study, are further connected with the conditions under which 'raw data' are obtained in the two disciplines. The peculiarly isolated position of the field-worker, be he ethologist or social anthropologist, must be remembered. One problem they share is that of accurately communicating findings which frequently cannot be easily checked, in a language often

---

[1] Cf. Rowell's remarks (1967) on the methodology of primate studies; 'One regularly encounters elderly baboons in the wild whose teeth are worn level with the gums, but which are well able to follow the daily routine of the troop. Such animals must be well over twenty years old at a very conservative estimate. Environments at the present are changing very rapidly; and animals with this sort of life span could live through great changes in habitat ... The field student coming into a new environment naturally tends to assume it is stable in its present state, and so finds difficulty in interpreting the behaviour of primate troops which are in part influenced by the past experience of their old members.'

[2] Tinbergen 1948.

[3] Hirsch, Lindley and Tolman 1955.

[4] Lorenz 1965. (1966 edn., p. 100.)

ill-adapted to the purpose.[1] We can accordingly ask whether the concepts of 'ethogram' and 'ethnography' (in the sense of 'an ethnography') are analogues in any sense. Both 'ethogram' and 'ethnography' represent the predominantly descriptive aspect of the discipline which is held, by implication, to be partly separable from its other aspects and to form an indispensable point of departure for these other aspects. The correspondence between them is a historical one as well. I have noted that the earliest writers' approach was often anecdotal, speculative and embedded in whatever philosophical pose was current. Tinbergen writes of the early 'classical' ethologists' 'wish to return to an inductive start, to observation and description of the enormous variety of animal behaviour repertoires, and to the simple, though admittedly vague and general question: 'Why do these animals behave as they do?'[2] There are evident parallels with Malinowski's insistence on the importance of starting with detailed and accurate fieldwork.

But in both disciplines it is recognized that this separation of analysis from observation is largely one of emphasis. It is worth giving representative definitions of both 'ethogram' and 'ethnography', coupled with views on the place of each concept in the total discipline:

The major premiss of ethology is that the study of animal behaviour must begin by obtaining as complete a knowledge as possible of the behaviour of the species in question during the entire life cycle . . . an ethogram . . . simply describes what an animal does, not why it does it. This goes beyond the usual naturalistic approach, since the various behaviours are then classified and compared with those of any other species, particularly related ones . . . The next step is their analysis in the light of the factors entering into or influencing these behaviours.[3]

At the present time the term 'ethnography' is fairly consistently used in anthropological literature to refer to descriptive studies of human societies, usually (though not necessarily) those so-called 'primitive' societies which are at a relatively simple level of political and economic development. Even descriptive studies must, however, imply some generalization, and since the theoretical framework employed in social anthropology has been developed in the past half-century, much recent

---

[1] Cf. Carpenter's discussion (1965, pp. 255–7) of the problems of a primatologist in the field. 'The question must be asked: Who made the observations, reports and inferences and what were his qualifications for making them?'

[2] Tinbergen 1963.   [3] Hess 1962.

ethnographic writing . . . is inevitably largely theoretical . . . modern social anthropologists are generally their own ethnographers . . .[1]

What we have uncovered, in considering analogies between the terms 'ethogram' and 'ethnography', is clearly a question about the possibility of 'pure' observation/description in the two disciplines concerned. Naturally, it does not follow that such an activity ever takes place, from the fact that both social anthropologists and ethologists make a broad distinction between the descriptive and analytic phases of their work. Evans-Pritchard remarks: 'I suppose that no-one would dispute that there is no other method in social anthropology than observation, classification and comparison in one form or another'[2], and Hinde, in a list of 'ethological methods' he believes to be of value in contexts outside the scope of ethology, places at the top 'the necessity for observation, description and classification before analysis'.[3] Tinbergen is a little worried about the ratio of observation to analysis in ethology, but concludes that there is ample room for both. '. . . we must, by a balanced development of our science, make sure that we attract the greatest possible variety of talent, and certainly not discourage the man with a gift for observation . . .'[4]

But it can be equally argued that any attempt at a full description of either social relations or species-specific behaviour, presupposes an explanation of the causal and other relations between the events and processes which make up the system. 'It is easy to think that describing a social class is like describing a man's clothes; but it is not. It is more like describing how his clothes are cleaned and pressed and returned to him with a bill.'[5]

Brown has expressed one view of the relations between observing, describing, reporting, classifying and so forth in a social context; interestingly, he uses a comparison between biological and social science in order to make his point. It is not suggested that all social anthropologists or ethologists, even in their capacity as authors of ethnographies and ethograms, would wish to identify themselves with Brown's 'natural historian'. But it is a rôle which either could reasonably choose to take up. I therefore quote Brown's analysis as a helpful starting-point for any ethologist or social anthropologist who feels the need to define this particular slice of his professional activity.

[1] Beattie 1964.   [2] Evans-Pritchard 1965.
[3] Hinde 1959.   [4] Tinbergen 1963.   [5] Brown 1963, p. 24.

The border zone between the history of natural events and the sciences of natural events is occupied by the study known as 'natural history'. There is a similar zone between the studies concerned with human history and the studies we call the 'social sciences' . . . 'the natural history of society.'

In general, the natural historian is concerned with reporting and describing rather than theoretical explanation. He identifies, classifies and describes what he observes . . . The perfect bird-watcher, then, is the perfect natural historian.

. . . Now the social analogue of the bird-watcher is the social observer. The social observer has the same pre-occupation with observing, reporting, classifying and describing; he has the same diminished interest in conducting experiments, and in producing laws and theories which fit into a body of scientific knowledge. The natural historian of human society resembles the natural scientist in that unlike the historian he has no particular concern with actions of the past as distinct from those of the present. Neither has he any special concern with problems of dating or questions of tracing social developments. On the other hand, the natural historian of human society resembles the ordinary historian in that both try to establish 'true statements about particular events, processes and situations'. The social observer is satisfied if he can show that a particular custom exists to a specified degree in a given society or that a particular cause operates . . . Thus it is not correct to say that natural historians are not interested in causal explanations. They are; what does not interest them are *general* explanations, ones which account for all cases of a certain type, rather than merely this case or that case.[1]

This, then, might offer for both social anthropology and ethology one way of marking off an 'observational' segment of the discipline from its other segments—although the fit is by no means exact, especially as regards general causal statements. Brown is probably right in characterizing the 'natural historian', whether of animal behaviour or human societies, as relatively uninterested in—or even suspicious of—an experimental methodology[2]. Yet there is a place in both ethology and social anthropology for the 'natural experiment'. By this is meant observing what happens to a total situation when one or a few well-defined elements of it are altered, either systematically by the observer himself or by some external agency, in a setting which by its nature is not amenable to rigorous control.[3] In Chapter VI (p. 95) I give a

[1] ibid., pp. 34–5.
[2] This is not to suggest that ethology as a whole is non-experimental.
[3] 'Control' in either of the two scientific senses of the word.

good example of the 'natural experiment' in social anthropology. Tinbergen is one exponent of the 'natural experiment' in ethology.[1]

Discussions of 'the comparative method' are found fairly frequently in both ethological and anthropological literature. I would suggest, however, that as a methodological parallel this is of limited interest. The expression 'comparative method' may indicate a certain uniformity of approach; but it would be rash to equate comparisons across species with comparisons across institutions or societies within a species, without first having established at what points the data themselves are comparable. In other words, comparisons between a's with respect to x and comparisons between b's with respect to y, can be relevant to one another only as far as x and y are themselves comparable kinds of thing (a good example of this problem emerges in Chapter VII, over the concept of 'greeting'). Nor have ethologists and social anthropologists, in their use of 'the comparative method' had the same aims in view. The former, it seems, are after 'tentative descriptions of the course evolution has taken'[2]; the latter, traditionally, the establishment of law-like propositions in sociology to match those of the natural sciences.[3] Evans-Pritchard gives good reasons for anthropologists' widespread dissatisfaction with 'the comparative method' if taken to be 'a method' rather than the necessary and desirable state of mind in which to approach one's material. His statement of its limitations comes strikingly close to that of Hinde and Tinbergen:

The method of statistical correlation can only pose questions; it cannot give us the answers to them.[4]

Comparative study itself cannot contribute directly to solution of this problem [the dynamics of behaviour evolution] but as a phase of research it is indispensable; it alone can supply us with a formulation of the problems to be solved.[5]

---

[1] See e.g. Tinbergen et al. 1962; and Tinbergen 1963 for a discussion of the limitations of this experiment. Another example, more directly comparable to the anthropological case above, is cited in Tinbergen 1953 (p. 136). Heinroth observed 'a swan attacking its mate when the latter's head happened to be submerged' indicating that 'the characters which allow individual recognition must be located in the head.'

[2] Hinde (1959) expands this view; and spells out the importance of a comparative approach: '(a) in facilitating observation, (b) in elucidating the evolution of behaviour, (c) in taxonomy, (d) in providing a basis for generalization, (e) in leading to an understanding of function.'

[3] See e.g. Evans-Pritchard 1963.   [4] ibid.   [5] Hinde and Tinbergen 1958.

A related problem concerns the relative desirability of the wide-ranging, general, essentially qualitative account and the narrower, essentially quantitative one. (This does not rule out the 'qualitative' exposition of a limited range of data. The point is the extent of generalization possible from the account; and this seems likely to bear an inverse relation to the degree of quantitative-ness). This problem does seem genuinely present in both disciplines; and the following statement of Hinde's about ethology could equally well be made, *mutatis mutandis*, of social anthropology:

The framework of ethological ideas can thus include both purely qualitative analysis of broad categories of behaviour . . . where the results are likely to have a fairly general validity, and more detailed analyses of particular problems, where the precise quantitative results are relevant only to the problem in hand (though of course they may point the way to less precise but broader generalizations). Both types of approach are necessary for an understanding of animal behaviour.[1]

I suggested above that the opposition wild/domesticated in ethology may be closely analogous to that of traditional/Westernized in social anthropology. Two further concepts seem to hold equally parallel significance; 'ethnocentrism' for social anthropology and 'anthropomorphism' for ethology. To begin with, each represents perhaps the most explicit procedural caveat of the appropriate discipline, and as a corollary each probably constitutes a prime focus of academic anxiety. Both concepts, nevertheless, are surprisingly difficult to pin down. Ethnocentrism according to Hoebel[2] has as its primary meaning the 'view of things in which one's own group is the centre of everything, and all others are scaled and rated with reference to it'—and is frequently used in this sense in (for example) the study of attitudes and personality. But crude ethnocentrism in an evaluative sense is less of a threat to the social anthropologist than is the epistemological danger of an 'ethnocentric' bias' in his treatment of the data. Hoebel quotes McIver and Page: 'The student of social life must be on constant guard against ethnocentric bias in analysing the ways of different groups; to this extent he must follow the principle of cultural relativity in his sociological investigations.'[3] But, the author goes on to say, the field-worker must allow himself a 'limited degree' of ethnocentrism in order to take up any kind of position in relation

[1] Hinde 1959.   [2] Hoebel 1964.   [3] ibid.

to what he observes. There is room of course for much discussion on whether a doctrine of cultural relativism is the only —or even a desirable—alternative to an ethnocentrically tinged view of societies.[1]

There is correspondingly some disagreement, or even confusion, among ethologists on what anthropomorphism really means. The condemnation of anthropomorphism in ethology is commonly understood to be a warning against ascribing 'subjective experiences' to animals and using a mentalistic language to do so. The most telling argument seems to be that '. . . for epistemological reasons . . . no such attempt can be considered scientific.'[2] What is not made clear is how attributing or not attributing 'subjective experience' to an animal is related to the aim of 'understanding' its behaviour in the broadest possible manner; much as in the case of ethnocentrism we were not told how we are to 'understand' a society without mistakenly imposing our own contingent cultural categories on it. Hediger (who admittedly may wish to distinguish between 'animal psychology' and ethology) claims that:

Those behaviour students who regard the animal not only as a thing, an object as it were, but also as a sentient and acting being, a subject whose behaviour can be understood more or less personally, just as one man understands another, these are the true animal psychologists. Animal psychology may thus be described as the investigation of behaviour, plus sympathetic understanding.[3]

Yet elsewhere he has stated that 'animal psychology, in the main, is a fight against anthropomorphizing the animal.'[4] Either he has simply changed his mind, or there is something obscure about his concept of anthropomorphism. Similarly Bierens de Haan, while rejecting a rigidly objective approach in the sense of a denial of subjective experiences in animals, certainly condemns anthropomorphism in *some* sense. He recounts that after Aristotle there developed two distinct lineages of thinking on the animal psyche: the Cartesian line which led to the modern Watsonian behaviourists and another which, via Darwin and the anecdotal evolutionists,

---

[1] Cf. Freeman 1965.

[2] Lorenz 1956. Cf. Tinbergen 1951, p. 4: 'Because subjective phenomena cannot be observed objectively in animals, it is idle either to claim or to deny their existence.' A remarkably solipsist argument, surely.

[3] Hediger 1955, p. 2.   [4] Hediger 1965.

generated 'an anthropomorphizing of the animal and an over-estimation of its psychic capacities.'[1]

One easily discerns, behind the discussions of both anthropomorphism and ethnocentrism, a concern about the meaning of 'objectivity' in observing human societies or species-specific behaviour, as the case may be. The idea of objectivity is, like the other concepts discussed above, difficult to define; especially so in social anthropology where the objectivity one is aiming for may depend on the particular variety of subjective bias one is trying to avoid. Thus the concept of objectivity may not always be a particularly illuminating contrast to that of ethnocentrism. But Lienhardt[2] has put forward an idea of objectivity in the sense of 'understanding the other man's point of view', and something comparable, viz. 'understanding the animal's point of view', evidently lies behind much of the discussion of subjective awareness in animals.[3] Huxley, for example, maintains that:

It is . . . both scientifically legitimate and operationally necessary to ascribe mind, in the sense of subjective awareness, to higher animals . . . We just cannot understand or properly interpret the behaviour of elephants or dogs or cats or porpoises unless we do so to some extent in mental terms. This is not anthropomorphism; it is merely an extension of the principles of comparative study that have been so fruitful in comparative anatomy, comparative physiology, comparative cytology and other biological fields. It is equally fruitful when you extend it to the study of animal behaviour, this new branch of science which we now call ethology.[4]

As far as ethology is concerned, it may be helpful to view those who allow and those who forbid taking into account the 'subjective experiences' of animals, as continuing (this time off the ideological plane) the old controversy about whether or not one erects a firm epistemological barrier between the understanding of human and of animal behaviour. Procedurally, the problem of objectivity is thrown back on the observer, and has its analogue in social anthro-

[1] Bierens de Haan 1948.Thus, glancing back to Chapter II, it can be argued that the early ethologists who rejected the methodology of 'mental evolutionism' were not innovating but rather taking up once more the dormant Cartesian tradition.
[2] Lienhardt 1963.
[3] Cf. von Uexküll's conception of the 'Umwelt' or perceptual world.
[4] Huxley 1962. See also Hume's remarks 'in praise of anthropomorphism' (1959).

pology. How much can the subjective and often non-communicable components of field-work be allowed to contribute to the observer's assessment of what he sees? The distinction is a tricky one for both ethologists and social anthropologists to make: between sympathetic open-mindedness towards their objects of study on the one hand and on the other, the 'if I were a horse' type of thinking whereby the observer enters empathically into a situation and risks illicitly imposing his own Gestalt on it.

It would not be particularly useful to discuss whether a general objectivity can actually be achieved in ethology or social anthropology. But one thing at least must be crucially important in both fields: to know whether one is deceiving oneself about the objectivity of the initial selection of data—the 'classification which precedes comparison'. Here too, ethnocentric and anthropomorphic bias present parallel stumbling-blocks, equally difficult (it may be impossible) to overcome. Evans-Pritchard[1] gives this as one of the principal reasons for the failure of 'the comparative method' in social anthropology as this method was traditionally conceived. Ethologists too surely need to be aware that there is a corresponding problem in their field. Tinbergen has indeed acknowledged its existence in some areas:

Concepts such as 'play' and 'learning' have not yet been purged completely of their subjectivist, anthropomorphic undertones. Both terms have not yet been satisfactorily defined objectively... both may well lump phenomena on the one hand, and exclude other phenomena on the other hand (and thus confuse the issue by a false classification) simply because the concepts are directly derived from human experience.[2]

Other criticisms have been more wholehearted. Kennedy for example argues that the traditional ethological models are subjective in that the concept of ethological 'energy' is itself drawn from human experience in rather a muddled way. He goes on: 'The kinship between ethology and Freud ... lies in their dualism ... what Lorenz has managed to do is to win wide acceptance among zoologists for the wholly subjective concepts of psycho-analysis.'[3]

[1] Evans-Pritchard 1963.
[2] Tinbergen 1963. Cf. Haldane's comments on Lorenz's paper (1956, Discussion, p. 64). 'Je doute que M. Lorenz ait le droit de se dire objectiviste tandis qu'il emploie des mots comme 'prying, etc ...' qui sont assez anthropomorphiques. Je ne suis pas d'ailleurs très hostile à l'anthropomorphisme, qui est une forme primitive de l'éthologie comparée.'
[3] Kennedy 1954.

I cannot help suspecting that (despite Tinbergen's token admission) ethologists tend to be a little complacent about the basis of their initial labelling of phenomena. This is not entirely a fair criticism, because however they come by their vocabulary ethologists certainly are strenuously concerned to know exactly what elements of behaviour they are talking about. Within the traditional confines of the discipline, probably no great harm is done.[1] The danger lies precisely in the area of this discussion; i.e. the basis on which one can validly compare human and animal cases. I have already commented on some ethologists' persistent habit of pronouncing loftily on human society. What one tends to get is a double thrill of recognition, or 'aha!-reaction'—'aha! here's an animal being territorial (or dominant)', 'aha! human beings are territorial (or dominant) as well.' Hence human societies, by implication, are to be understood in ethological terms, Q.E.D. Concealed premiss: that we know and can recognize territoriality or dominance in animals without having drawn on our own workaday model of society in the first place. It is worth considering whether the concept of 'ritualization' as introduced by Huxley (1914) is a prime example of the 'aha!-reaction'. The reaction doubles back on itself in the standard manner, so that we are now asking ourselves the possibly misleading question 'what is the relationship between ritualization and ritual?' (. . . between territoriality and nationalism? . . . between dominance and authority?). If this is indeed what has been happening, it obscures but does not alter the strong probability that *something* comparable can be discovered in both human and animal cases. I leave till Chapter IX the question how this 'something' is to be approached.

No one would claim that the above remarks radically affect the validity of the huge body of impressive material that ethologists produce and have produced. But it may be suggested that a broad interdisciplinary approach such as I am advocating might persuade them to re-open one or two questions which have traditionally been regarded as closed.

THE LEVEL OF DATA

This 'level', and the two to follow, will be discussed far less lengthily than the 'level' of procedure above. This is because the

[1] But some would hold that *any* failure to recognize one's own assumptions is harmful.

latter stands largely on its own, while the former point forward to later chapters (and, far more important, to future research); raising issues which can only be evaluated in the light of evidence on specific topics.

This level of data, then, covers the search for things common (in some sense) to human and animal social life. Now it is very easy to speak of 'continuities', 'constants', 'parallels' and so forth in the workings of human and animal societies; and at certain stages of the analytic process these are not hard to find. It requires no great effort of understanding, for example, to see that a territorial principle in some form is followed by a great many species and is also found in human societies (but beware the 'aha!-reaction', discussed above). It is more difficult to decide exactly what meaning we can attach to these obvious comparisons, and to work out a vocabulary more precise than that of 'continuities' and 'parallels'. Ardrey has stated one of the problems rather well: '. . . while we may pursue without end certain parallels between animal and human behaviour, there will remain always the chance that what we observe in man is a kind of mirror held up to nature: our culture and our learning reflect the natural way without in a biological sense being beholden to it.'[1] Leaving aside the doubtful contrast between the 'natural way' and any other, one may feel that Ardrey is unduly pessimistic (for once) in claiming that the question is forever open. Clearly it is very important indeed to know in what ways there can be 'real' connections between events and processes which 'look the same' (and may owe their apparent relatedness to a deceptive terminology). Even if Ardrey is right, we can always step back and ask how it comes about that human social life resembles that of animals (if indeed it does) in such a mirror-like fashion.

A further difficulty (which scarcely needs pointing out) is that at this, as at every other level, one must beware of naïvely comparing 'human' with 'animal' cases as if the latter represented some kind of unitary category. There might be minimal grounds for such an assumption if one accepted the ideological or epistemological barriers between the human and animal world, discussed above and in Chapters II and III. But even here, the 'animal' category is defined only by exclusion and gives no positive unity. I have, it is true, used this kind of expression throughout in a shorthand

[1] Ardrey 1966, p. 103.

manner; but it must be understood as a shorthand and nothing more. Unique as man may be, there are deep differences between one animal group and another, which must not be obscured by a false simplification. Ethologists are nearly always most careful about cross-specific generalizations, relating them to broadly-based taxonomic principles.

A related but more subtle difficulty is that of comparing the behaviour of widely differing species where the techniques of observation, interpretation and verification appropriate to each may also be very different. For example Crook, commenting on Reynolds' theory of the course of hominoid evolution, makes the following criticism:

Reynolds' tendency has been to look upon these social relations as if they were 'fixed action patterns' of the type found in bird courtship. The use of a kind of reasoning found in classical ethology in the context of mammalian behaviour at the hominid level is not only extremely mis-leading to the non-zoologist but is also to put such behaviour in the wrong category.[1]

The problem might be partially solved by comparing species with one another on the basis of their rating on certain dimensions which are claimed to be analytic. Whether or not they are analytic is difficult to decide, especially (for the reasons discussed above) if one wishes to include the possibility of human comparisons. But Klopfer and Hailman, for example, adopt this procedure:

The organisation of animal societies can be attributed to four principal kinds of behaviour patterns . . . the behaviour associated with territori-ality and the maintenance of individual distance, with dominance relations, with leadership and with parental care and mutual stimulation. With the possible exception of the rigidly demarcated insect societies, it is possible to arrange social organisations according to the degree to which one or the other of these patterns predominates.[2]

More broadly, the biological concepts of homology, analogy and convergence may go some way towards helping us out of these difficulties. The anthropologists and others who have recently been showing interest in the biological elements of human society, have mainly focused their attention on possible homologous links between the social life of man and of the primates and putative

[1] Crook 1967.   [2] Klopfer and Hailman 1967, p. 141.

early hominids. This kind of investigation clearly rests on evidence of primate evolution, and not being qualified to evaluate such evidence I shall not comment further on it.[1]

But I do not believe that the search for points at which animal findings become relevant to problems of human society, commits us to establishing that the cases being compared are homologously linked in a direct fashion. (This is not to forget that 'homology' is relative to taxonomic level; obviously, man has primate characteristics, mammal characteristics etc.) We also have the possibilities of convergence, in a more or less rigorous sense. Strictly speaking, perhaps, the judgement that two structures or behaviour patterns in different species owe their similarity to convergent or analogical evolution rather than to common phylogenetic origins relies on evidence that common selection pressures have been exerted on each species by environmental conditions or by the logic of the situation. Thus:

... food hiding in very different species might at first look homologous but the similarity would actually be due to function, as there are only a few ways in which food can be stored. Such analogy of behaviour is more likely, furthermore, when similar behaviour patterns are to be found in different species whose mode of living is the same (tree nesting, seed eating) or that live in the same biotope ... but which have relatives in other biotopes and with a different manner of living, and therefore lacking these particular behaviour patterns.[2]

This 'logic of the situation' could form the basis of our model for comparing human social life with that of even vastly different species such as the jackdaw or herring-gull, where common selection pressures cannot be guessed at and it would be nonsense to speak of comparable living conditions. What is needed at this level of data is a certain degree of abstraction in dealing with remotely related species, a receptivity towards common 'themes' and structures running through the data. This point of view should not be alien to the social anthropologist; it is after all not essentially different from the procedure followed by van Gennep, and latterly by Mary Douglas.[3] In Chapters v, vi, vii and viii I set out to work through some of the data on selected topics. What things actually occur in both human and animal social life, and how

[1] But see e.g. Geertz 1964; Hockett and Ascher 1964; Reynolds 1966; Sahlins 1959 and 1960; Spuhler 1959.
[2] Hess 1962.   [3] See Douglas 1966.

they may be characterized, I hope may begin to emerge in the process. These ideas will be taken up again in the concluding chapter.

THE LEVEL OF THEORY

At this level the appropriate questions have to do with the consequences, for the theoretical bases of both disciplines, of acknowledging the linkages between them sketched above and worked out more fully in the chapters to follow. In this inquiry, the predominant interest is in the direction of ethological comparisons having consequences for social anthropology, rather than the other way round. But the ethological cases which are at all relevant for this purpose, are likely to be precisely those which point to a possible 'sociology' of certain animal species. Hence a big question comes up at this level: whether we shall in the end be able to reach some 'minimal' definition of sociology which will isolate those areas and points of analysis where animal and human social organizations may be comparable with one another. Any possibility that emerges in this way of validly extending 'sociological thinking' to the animal world will, presumably, be of some interest to ethologists.

To return to the opposite standpoint; one could ask, crudely, what an 'ethologized anthropology' would look like—and if there is an answer it can only be a retrospective one. Part of the problem may be expressed by asking whether one could write an ethogram of the human species. The answer is that if this were tried it would look suspiciously like an ethnography of a very exhaustive kind, or else it would lack any reference at all.[1] Naïve re-description of human behaviour in ethological language is a popular technique among ethologists who feel that their methods and results can help us to understand our own social processes. Morris's *The Naked Ape*[2] is an excellent example of this. But in fact one has to look quite hard to find an actually naked 'naked ape'. There is, it seems, good reason to believe that *Homo sapiens* is genetically committed to the 'clothes' of culture,[3] and Morris, by stripping

---

[1] Cf. the precisely parallel fate of the concept of a 'culturally defined personality', discussed in Chapter 1.

[2] Morris 1967.

[3] See Geertz 1964 and cf. Lenneburg's argument (1964) that 'language specialization need not mystify us' because 'language is due to as yet unknown species-specific biological capacities.'

him of all this in imagination, misses every possible point. Lear naked in the storm is no man; and to say of persons (I use the word deliberately) that 'the vast majority of all copulatory activity ... occurs when the partners are in a pair-bonded state ...'[1] is not to describe anything at all. This may be contrasted with Lorenz's belief—probably true—that the configurations 'short face in relation to a large forehead, protruding cheeks, maladjusted limb movements' act as sign stimuli releasing parental responses in a wide range of species, including our own.[2] I do not think we gain much from pretending to be Martians, except a certain amount of fun and, perhaps, an illusion that our perceptions are less bounded than they are.

The Naked Ape exemplifies one strategy for reconciling the vocabulary of ethology with that appropriate to human society (namely, the strategy of ignoring the latter) and I believe that it is an abortive one. But clearly, the problem is not one of vocabulary alone. If anthropologists think fit to take professional notice of the findings and formulations of ethology, then they will have somehow to accommodate the prevailing theoretical standpoint of ethologists—which is, overwhelmingly, that of general modern evolutionary theory. Nor have they been unaware of this. Tiger and Fox, as we have seen (p. 25), wish to see the study of human social life subsumed within a general zoology of behaviour.[3] Whatever this means, it evidently involves more than the 'naïve human ethogram' type of effort I have just criticized. I have commented in Chapter III on the dangers of applying a theory of natural selection too uncritically to human societies. The rôle of evolutionary theory in social anthropology is too broad a topic to be tackled in this work, and is accordingly sidestepped. But it may be said in passing that Huxley has made a promising start by abstracting from the details of evolutionary change to 'mechanisms of maintenance, transmission and transformation' and by recommending that the 'biological and psycho-social sectors' of evolution be brought together at this level.[4]

On the basis of evidence set out in Chapters V, VI, VII and VIII, I hope to show that certain traditional assumptions of British social anthropology, in particular the privileged status of the 'social fact' as an exclusively human phenomenon, could do with some revising.

---

[1] Morris 1967, p. 62. [2] Cited in Tinbergen 1951, p. 209.
[3] Tiger and Fox 1966. [4] Huxley 1955 and 1958.

This will follow, I believe, from acceptance of the value and interest of ethological comparisons. But it may be a matter for 'pedagogic' decision whether or not to admit such comparisons; whether or not to preserve social anthropology as a relatively closed system at this theoretical level. Whether this option remains open, or whether it is true that the 'data force us into a position of readiness', I am unable to say.

THE PRAGMATIC LEVEL

It seems reasonable to suppose that an understanding of those features of human behaviour that are 'instinctive' in some sense, and of whatever elements of 'social structure' we share with other social species, may be of value in recognizing and coping with actual problems of social organization. Problems of aggression and of population control immediately suggest themselves (see Chapters v and vi). Apart from this, there are a number of indirect pragmatic links between ethology and anthropology or sociology, via psychiatry and social medicine.[1] The relevance of imprinting to problems of child-rearing, for example, is a well-attested case.[2] Hinde has given a sensible summary of the basis on which animal findings can shed light on human mental disorder, and hence (one may conclude) on principles of social administration best fitted to forestall such disorder:

. . . the study of animals can help in the study of human neurosis, but this help cannot be derived from a simple comparison of pathological behaviour in animals and man. Rather, the greater simplicity of behaviour in animals makes possible an analysis of the manner in which neurotic symptoms are established. The very existence of symptoms in animals, comparable to those seen in man, suggests that their occurrence in man does not necessarily demand explanations specific to the human case; though man's greater use of conceptual thought often permits more tenuous connections between conflict and symptoms than can ever occur in animals.[3]

Finally, a question of social responsibility comes up for anyone investigating pragmatic links between a 'sociology' of animals and of men. I said in Chapter III (p. 23) that if we admit linkages between these two disciplines at the level of data, we may have to accept

[1] See e.g. Barnett (ed.) 1962.
[2] See e.g. Gray 1958 and Hinde 1961.   [3] Hinde 1962.

certain limitations on the possibilities of social change. It is naturally most important to find out exactly where these limitations lie, and how compelling they are. It may be, for example, that we can get around them by borrowing techniques 'designed' at the animal level for this very purpose—as Lorenz believes that we can overcome the problem of aggression in society by ritualizing and redirecting it in harmless ways. To reveal that something dangerous, such as aggression, is an inescapable biologically guaranteed fact of human social existence, and to abandon the question there with an air of duty done, may well count as an abdication of intellectual responsibility. It may also lead to a false (because ill-informed) determinism comparable to the crudest excesses of the Social Darwinists.

It will be seen that the four 'levels' I have outlined cannot be kept separate, but merge inextricably in the treatment which follows of certain specific topics. But I think these distinctions have been helpful; I shall return to them in my concluding appraisals of the programme in Chapter IX.

V

ON REGULATING THE SIZE OF GROUPS

As is clear from the title of this chapter, its theme overlaps greatly with the general study of population control. The latter, needless to say, involves a wide range of specialist fields (such as population genetics) which are outside the scope and competence of this work. This chapter is exclusively concerned with questions about the regulation of numbers through social structure and behaviour, and whether it is in any way appropriate to look for comparable regulating processes in human and animal cases. I shall go about this by first commenting on certain recent publications on the subject (in particular the work of Wynne-Edwards and Mary Douglas) and then pointing to certain wider issues which this discussion throws up.

I use the term 'groups' in preference to 'populations' because the former indicates more accurately the questions which I propose to take as open. On a homeostatic theory such as that put forward by Wynne-Edwards, the identity of a population (for the purposes of group-selection, for example) is defined by this very characteristic of self-regulation; and in a sense the phrase 'population control' becomes a tautology. But in considering this as a possible area of contact between ethology and social anthropology one of the crucial questions is, given that there are populations in this sense, whether there are any in human societies—in other words, whether a comparable 'homeostatic machine' could operate in the latter case. I take the word 'group' as neutral and free from any implication of homeostasis. The word 'population' too suggests a largeish collection of individuals, with more or less permanent boundaries; groups on the other hand can be defined *ad hoc* and can even be momentary, and can have shifting boundaries. It seems no less appropriate to look for self-regulating systems in groups, than in populations in the commonly understood sense, although the actual mechanisms may be quite different in a short-term, small-scale situation. Reynolds[1] has recently suggested that one effect of

[1] Reynolds 1966.

the development of hierarchical social systems, both in captive primate groups and (conjecturally) in early man living for the first time in settled communities, is to control the frequency and intensity of effective face-to-face contacts in an essentially over-crowded situation. Leyhausen[1] has shown that the more cats are crowded and confined, the more 'dominance-minded' they become; this could be an instance of the same thing. Calhoun's[2] work on rodents exhibits further the dire consequences of causing the limits on actual social contact to break down completely. This idea of 'effective face-to-face contact', ill-defined though it is at present, is likely to be an important one in the analysis of groups of what-ever kind and scale; and one may guess that a principle of self-regulation of numbers, if it operates at all, could operate at a variety of levels and of time-scales.

One reason why I have taken this as the first of my four selected topics is that it has been much discussed in the past—more so than any of them except 'aggression' and more sensitively even than that. Carr-Saunders devotes the first chapter of his *The Population Problem*[3] to a historical survey of theories of population control, to which the reader is referred. Darwin, despite his prejudiced view of 'low savages', clearly anticipates in *The Descent of Man* several of the issues which concern writers such as Mary Douglas today. Halsey[4] says that Darwin took over Malthus' ecological but not his preventative, or sociological, checks on population growth; this is just not true, and it is worth quoting Darwin at some length in order to establish this.

The primary or fundamental check to the continued increase of man is the difficulty of *gaining subsistence, and of living in comfort* . . . With civilized nations this primary check acts chiefly by restraining marriages. [he adds that infant mortality, epidemics, war and emigration also play a certain part] . . . Notwithstanding that savages appear to be less prolific than civilized people, they would no doubt rapidly increase if their numbers were not by some means rigidly kept down . . . Savages almost always marry; yet there is some prudential restraint, for they do not commonly marry at the earliest possible age. The young men are often required to show that they can support a wife: they have in general first to earn the price with which to purchase her from her parents . . . Malthus has discussed these several checks, but he does not lay stress

---

[1] Leyhausen 1965.   [2] See e.g. Calhoun 1962.
[3] Carr-Saunders 1922.   [4] Halsey 1967.

enough on what is probably the most important of all, namely infanticide, especially of female infants, and the habit of procuring abortion . . . If we look back to an extremely remote epoch, before man had arrived at the dignity of manhood, he would have been guided more by instinct and less by reason than are the lowest savages at the present time. Our early semi-human progenitors would not have practised infanticide or polyandry; for the instincts of the lower animals are never so perverted as to lead them regularly to destroy their own offspring, or to be quite devoid of jealousy . . . the progenitors of man would have tended to increase rapidly, but checks of some kind, whether periodical or constant, must have kept down their numbers, even more severely than with existing savages. What the precise nature of these checks were, we cannot say, any more than with most other animals.[1]

Carr-Saunders held a fairly simple view of the relation between the 'population problem' in animal and in human groups. He distinguished between the 'qualitative' and 'quantitative' aspects of the problem; and claimed that in both these respects the problem is virtually the same for all species, including early primitive man, living in 'a state of nature'.

The ancestors of man were at one time subject to the same conditions from which they have, step by step, moved away owing to the development of the faculty of reason. We have to trace the causes and results of this moving away—of the progressive modifications of the conditions existing among species in a state of nature.[2]

Thus Carr-Saunders differs from Darwin chiefly in implying that the nature of the problem, as well as the ways in which it can be solved, is radically altered once rationality is achieved. This is understandable in view of Carr-Saunders' optimistic view of the demographic future of mankind.

THE WYNNE-EDWARDS/MARY DOUGLAS EXCHANGE

Wynne-Edwards in his recent book *Animal Dispersion in Relation to Social Behaviour*[3] has cast a direct challenge from modern biology to modern social science. The first thing to note about Wynne-Edwards is that even within his own field his theory of population homeostasis is a highly controversial one. Crook for example has attacked it on methodological grounds:

[1] Darwin 1871, pp. 44–7. My emphasis.
[2] Carr-Saunders 1922, p. 82.   [3] Wynne-Edwards 1962.

To support the thesis a mass of material that is not contradictory to the argument has been selected and examined. The theory is not therefore based primarily on induction from precise results—rather evidence is used which is found to support an *a priori* hypothesis. In developing the theory the premiss of an 'optimum 'population is often used as if it were a self-evident fact from which deductive inference may legitimately be made . . . by using certain postulates as assumptions, the theory acquires an appearance of greater solidity than in fact it has. The evidence used in support is in many cases explicable on other grounds and these are not at all excluded by the argument.[1]

Clearly we are not dealing with a case of something accepted and established in biology, waiting quietly for the attention of the social scientist. The details of Wynne-Edwards' theory, as far as they are relevant to the comparison of animal with human social life, are set out in Mary Douglas' article[2] and in Halsey's[3]. Very briefly, Wynne-Edwards interprets a good deal of animal social organization (practically the whole of it) as a crucial element in a vast homeostatic system which regulates the size and density of populations, keeping them below the level at which irreversible over-exploitation of the really critical resources of the environment might begin to occur. This view, he implies, must be taken into account by human social scientists, on pain of accusations of professional negligence. For example he defines a society as 'an organization capable of providing conventional competition . . . The existence of such societies is usually most clearly revealed . . . by the possession of methods of mutual communications and recognition, through conventional signs and signals given and received, which form an indispensable link in social integration.'[4] He means it too; he wishes to interpret periodical tribal gatherings among primitive peoples as furnishing the feedback element of the homeostatic machine. Midsummer festivals among American Indians, for example, 'appear to be the only possible source of what knowledge exists regarding changes in numbers in the population, and to be the basis, therefore, on which tribal customs relating to sexual abstinence, infanticide and other forms of birth-control are built up, reinforced and relaxed.'[5] He adds, it is true, that these gatherings have political, judicial and ritual functions as well; but there is no doubt which explanation is to be given

[1] Crook 1965.   [2] Douglas 1966a.   [3] Halsey 1967.
[4] Wynne-Edwards 1962, pp. 14–15.   [5] ibid., p. 219.

precedence. The relative positions of men and women in most societies are interpreted along the same lines: 'The emphasis on the male
sex as the heirs of wealth and position reinforces their pre-
existing epideictic responsibility and function, the womenfolk
remaining in this as in other respects largely as obligate depen-
dants.'[1] I have nothing against experimenting with biological
comparisons in studying the relation between the sexes in human
societies—and have indeed attempted just this in Chapter VIII. But
there is an important difference; my approach is (I claim) essentially
a structural one, rather than relying on a functional continuity
between animal and human cases—where the function in question
is by no means demonstrated for either.

For Wynne-Edwards, then, there is a bridge between animal
and human social organization and it is a functional one. Both are
concerned either actually or vestigially with a homeostatic mechanism of population control. It is only fair to add that Wynne-
Edwards is not centrally concerned with explanations of human
society. I place him in the category of those ethologists who, in
setting out their theories, add dogmatic but parenthetical riders
about the application of the theories to the human case. I have
searched the bibliography of *Animal Dispersion* and have found only
two purely ethnographic titles, dated 1922 and 1926. Wynne-
Edwards appears to rely on Carr-Saunders' authority in claiming
that abstention from intercourse, abortion and infanticide are
widely or universally practised in primitive societies. Since he came
across *The Population Problem* only after the draft of his own book
was complete,[2] one may guess that the homeostatic theory was
applied to human populations rather as an afterthought.

But if Wynne-Edwards makes no claim to anthropological
sophistication, his ideas certainly deserve the attention of those who
do. Mary Douglas is in broad agreement with Wynne-Edwards that
there are social mechanisms of restraint on population size in
human groups, with the proviso that not 'bread and butter' but
'oysters and champagne' are the limiting factors; i.e. it is prestige
which sets the target to the homeostatic machine. (The latter is my
phrasing of her view; she does not commit herself on the general
validity of a homeostatic model for societies.) She has two criticisms of Wynne-Edwards' theory—firstly that it is 'so protected

[1] ibid., p. 191.
[2] ibid., p. 21.

from contradictory evidence as to be irrefutable,' and secondly that the possibility of underpopulation is 'not seriously considered'. In human society, she says, many classes of activity require a minimum number of participants. In fact this is frequently the case among animal groups, which can have a minimal as well as a maximal size. It has been said that 'one chimpanzee is no chimpanzee' and that 'a baboon without its troop is a dead baboon'; and one has only to think of pack-hunters, or animals which depend on communal herding for defence against predators. So this is not in itself an argument against comparing human and animal cases.

The question of underpopulation is in my view less important than the issues into which it merges; such as the balance between 'conservatism' and 'pioneering' in populations, and the relation of this balance to the predictability of the environment. Wynne-Edwards does deal quite fully with these points, showing that 'a compromise is required between strict conservatism to the ancestral soil on the one hand, and a tendency to pioneer into unoccupied ground on the other.'[1] Hence this compromise, or a temporary stage in the working-out of it, might be mistaken for underpopulation. Of course there is no denying that 'true' underpopulation in both animal and human groups, in which the size of the groups falls far below the optimum in terms of yield per head even on a long-term view, can occur; Dr. Douglas' American Indian example seems to be a clear case of this. My point is an obvious one: that the question of underpopulation on a homeostatic model is not ultimately separable from the more general issue of the verifiability of the 'Principle of Optimum Number'. This is certainly the shakiest point in Wynne-Edwards' whole theory, even for animal populations, as is made clear in Crook's criticism which I quoted above. Wynne-Edwards himself is reduced to saying, a little weakly, that 'It seems quite possible, on the basis of general experience, that something approaching these conditions [of 'optimal' population size] may in fact often be realised.'[2] He holds the same to be true, though unprovable, of human populations in a 'primitive' state, and in saying so he reveals a rather touching, almost pre-Victorian, romanticism:

How can it be shown that primitive populations approximate to the optimum number? The answer is that it cannot be done conclusively,

[1] ibid., 463.   [2] ibid., p. 4.

but only by the indirect evidence that such people usually appear to approach the highest standard of living within their reach. The former conception of savages always in a state of semi-starvation is utterly false; they are commonly people of graceful proportions and beautiful physique, able to endure hardships it is true, but wonderfully equipped for the lives they lead; they enjoy good health and live to an advanced age.[1]

Thus in selecting underpopulation as an issue, Dr. Douglas skirts what I should regard as one of the crucial difficulties of Wynne-Edwards' theory, for both human and animal cases. But she rightly points out, of course, that in considering whether human societies achieve an optimum population size a far wider set of considerations become relevant—such as what the people are interested in, apart from their staple economy.

Dr. Douglas' other criticism, that of irrefutability, exhibits a curious element of double-think—a central slipperyness—in the theory as it is applied to human groups. For one can easily extract from Wynne-Edwards' book the view that it would be futile to look for homeostatic mechanisms in human societies at all (except perhaps in the most primitive and isolated groups) because the essential regulating processes have atrophied. Owing to man's accelerated achievement of control over the environment and efficiency in food-production, the self-regulating systems have long ago gone 'by default.'[2] He admits, as we have seen, the difficulty of showing that human populations (whether primitive or civilized) are or ever have been controlled at an 'optimal' level, and as we have seen, this same problem arises over the whole range of his zoological examples. Dr. Douglas could, if she chose, have followed this line and taken up a position in relation to Wynne-Edwards' claim that certain features of human social life are 'survivals' of a former set of dispersionary systems. This would have let us off the awkward anthropological hook, 'animals and primitive men have self-regulating systems of population control, which we civilized peoples lack.' On the other hand it is quite respectable to hold, as Dr. Douglas implicitly does (at least she does not deny it) that for rather unimportant reasons such as geographical isolation, many primitive groups are significantly more like the bounded, potentially immortal populations subject to group-selection with which the homeostasis theory deals, than are most 'civilized' groups.

Instead of following this line, however, Dr. Douglas allows the

[1] ibid., p. 494.   [2] ibid., p. 220.

fitness of looking for self-regulating systems in at least some present-day human groups—the above-quoted passage on p. 494 shows that this is a perfectly good alternative reading of Wynne-Edwards—and takes issue with him on the difficulty of choosing test cases. The double-think on Wynne-Edwards' part arises from the coincidence of both lines of thought. For we are brought dangerously near to the argument—not unknown in anthropology—that negative instances of a generalization are to be explained within the terms of the generalization itself—that a homeostatic process regulates the size of human groups except where it has stopped doing so. On all three counts, Dr. Douglas' charge of irrefutability is unanswerable. But as I have said, this criticism has been made of the theory as a whole, as well as its application to the human case, and is not an argument against the principle of applying a hypothesis, valid for animal groups, to human societies.

Both Wynne-Edwards and Mary Douglas curiously limit their consideration of the human case to controls on recruitment—indeed abstention from intercourse (and all kinds of contraception), abortion and infanticide seem traditionally to have been regarded as the principal agents of human population control. That Dr. Douglas feels that these measures represent the total range of human population control mechanisms which can be compared with those of animals, is suggested by her choice of examples. In three of her four cases—The Pelly Bay Eskimos, the Tikopia and the Nambudiri Brahmins—in the traditional society both emigration and immigration seem, for social and geographical reasons, to have been effectively ruled out. If in these cases we assume that the child and adult mortality rates were either fairly constant or randomly variable, then recruitment was presumably the only point at which controls could be expected to operate. In contrast, Russell and Russell have a theory[1] that in human as in animal groups increases in population pressure are responded to in a systematic and predictable manner; by increased 'social disorganization' and 'social tension' culminating in progressive weakening of the whole population as well as selective victimization of women and children. This could be regarded as a homeostatic mechanism of population control, but one which does not act only on recruitment.

A further guess from Dr. Douglas' choice of examples is that

[1] Russell and Russell 1968.

she is thinking primarily of controls acting at a level of rationality; of human societies 'consciously' (in some sense) limiting the size of their populations to accord with the supply of prestige-bearing resources. Now there is nothing in Wynne-Edwards' model to restrict its scope to non-rational processes. Indeed, he hints[1] that in human societies simple 'insight' may be the proximate density-dependent brake which halts population growth before the environment can be seriously and irreversibly 'over-fished'. The question naturally arises whether, and in what sense, rational processes in human and non-rational in animal groups can be brought within a single model. What we need is an analysis of the relation between rationality and natural selection as controllers of events—two sets of influences which Carr-Saunders, for one, places in opposition to one another. Until this is done (and it cannot be done here) we cannot get much further on this line of thought.

On the other hand, the fact that we are considering the possibility of social mechanisms of self-regulation in human groups, does not in itself restrict us to looking at action consciously directed to that end. Here, particularly, it is an advantage to think in terms of 'groups' rather than, more cumbersomely, of populations. For in a small-scale and short-term situation, certain non-conscious and collective processes may turn out to be closely analogous to dispersive mechanisms in animal social behaviour. The maintenance of individual distances, and a possible limitation on the number of people with whom one can interact in a given time at a given level of intensity, may come under this head. These points are discussed below.

Finally it may be suggested that on her own ground Dr. Douglas is more closely in agreement with Wynne-Edwards than she claims to be. She writes:

For the animal population it makes sense to make the calculation in terms of critical resources and to recognize that the critical resource is not necessarily food; it may be nesting room or some other necessary amenity. But for human behaviour it can be more relevant to take into account the ceiling imposed by the demand for champagne or private education than the demand for bread and butter.[2]

Might it not be that for the purposes of the theory, champagne and private education represent precisely the goals of conventional

[1] Wynne-Edwards 1962, pp. 542–3.   [2] Douglas 1966a.

competition which in Wynne-Edwards' view replace a free-for-all in exploiting the really critical resources; and that the demand for them actually corresponds rather closely to (say) the competition for status in a hierarchy which characterizes so many animal 'societies'? For example the availability of Jaguars and private education (or rather people's access to them) could quite conceivably act as a 'proximate' and in some complicated sense 'density-dependent' factor influencing emigration. Of course, whether the scarcity value of champagne bears any actual relation to the margin of safety before one begins 'over-fishing' the critical resource, is in every case open to question. In most modern societies it would be far-fetched even to postulate any such relation. And (to repeat Dr. Douglas' most telling argument) whatever behavioural systems there may be for large-scale human population control, in many cases they manifestly do not work. (Maybe they do not work because they *are* aimed at the recruitment phase—a system ill-designed for a long-lived, slow-maturing species with a relatively long interval between generations. The system would take a long while to respond to even sharp shifts in the 'target' of optimal population-size, and one would tend to get the kind of wild oscillation characteristic of cybernetic systems whose time-lag is too long. This will only become a problem when immigration and emigration are difficult or impossible—for these would clearly provide a more sensitive and immediate response to shifting pressures of population.)

MORE GENERAL QUESTIONS

The application to human society of a theory developed within ethology has not, in this particular case, been an unqualified success. But it is worth looking at one or two wider issues thrown up in the Wynne-Edwards/Mary Douglas exchange, in order to see whether Wynne-Edwards' failure to establish his case goes deeper than a failure of evidence and logic.

There are excellent precedents for the view that a theory of cybernetic homeostasis is applicable in the field of sociology; for no less an authority than Norbert Wiener was of this opinion. Towards the end of *Cybernetics* he wrote:

Thus small, closely knit communities have a very considerable measure of homeostasis . . . whether they are highly literate communities in a civilized country, or villages of primitive savages. Strange and even repugnant as the customs of many barbarians may seem to us, they generally have a very definite homeostatic value, which it is part of the function of anthropologists to interpret. It is only in the large community, where the Lords of Things as they Are protect themselves from hunger by wealth, from public opinion by privacy and anonymity, from private criticism by the laws of libel and the possession of the means of communication, that ruthlessness can reach its most sublime levels. Of all these anti-homeostatic factors in society, the control of the means of communication is the most effective and most important.[1]

There is undoubtedly a sense in which practically all the operations of society could be called homeostatic. Systems of 'social control' could be envisaged as error-activated devices which serve to bring people or their actions or the general state of things 'back' to some 'desired' condition. Homans defines 'social control' as: 'The process by which, if a man departs from his existing degree of obedience to a norm, his behaviour is brought back towards that degree, or would be brought back if he did depart.'[2] The difficulties arise when one begins to wonder what, in the case of societies, sets the 'target' to the homeostatic mechanism. This is no problem for physiological homeostasis as it relates to specific bodily systems such as that of temperature-regulation in a warm-blooded animal. The 'correct' temperature can be taken as 'given' by the organism's overall design; the job of the homeostatic mechanism is to maintain it with minimum fluctuations. Wynne-Edwards, as we have seen, wishes to extend the idea of homeostasis to include the self-regulation of populations by social behaviour. For him the corresponding 'target' which makes the analogy possible is furnished by a theoretically optimal population-size. Again as we have seen, there are difficulties about showing that either animal or human populations do actually tend to approach such an optimum. As far as the general organization of human societies is concerned, the analogy between physiological and 'social' homeostasis becomes even more doubtful. There is seldom any definable state of affairs to represent a 'target' of homeostatic control. For example the 'target' of social control in the sense of the machinery of criminal law cannot be 'things as they were before a given breach occurred' where crime is endemic; nor can it be 'a crime-less society' where there is no evidence of society

[1] Wiener 1948, p. 187.   [2] Homans (1960), in Wolff 1964.

actually tending towards this ideal. The idea that the physiological concept of homeostasis can be borrowed to provide general sociological explanations is, I suspect, plausible only on a rather old-fashioned view of societies, a view which over-stresses their conservatism and neglects the shifts, the ambiguities and the vaguenesses in people's conception of an 'ideal' or 'desired' state of affairs.

I feel then that we can do without the idea of 'homeostasis' as a general principle of human social organization, if this analogy brings with it the illusion that something precise has been uncovered. I reserve judgement on the question of population homeostasis on a large scale, for the reasons discussed above. It remains to be shown, I think, whether population homeostasis does occur in human societies around a 'target' related in some way to the supply of prestige-bearing commodities.

It would be interesting to find out, however, whether anything like self-regulation of numbers can occur in groups in a short-term, small-scale situation. We cannot get very far with this until we know much more about the significant parameters of everyday social behaviour (see Chapter VII). A good deal of work has been done by psychologists in roughly this field,[1] but it is of little value here because of its bias towards the techniques and motivations of the individual. What is needed for the present purpose is information about the systematic structuring of everyday behaviour at a supra-individual level. Certain findings provide circumstantial hints of what these 'parameters' might be; the work of Reynolds, Leyhausen and Calhoun has been cited above. The general idea seems to be that there is in ourselves and other social species some kind of optimal 'level' of total social contact; and this can be achieved by shifting either the frequency or the 'intensity' of actual encounters. Both Reynolds and Calhoun, from different standpoints, relate this suggestion to a possible source of the development of human culture. Calhoun writes

. . . so many species of mammals, up through the primates, live in compact groups of about twelve adults. By virtue of his biological heritage, *Homo Sapiens* appears to have been long related, and presumably adjusted to, a way of life that was most harmonious when the population was fragmented into small social groups of about twelve adults . . . Furthermore, I have shown that, when we increase the group size of rats above

[1] See e.g. Argyle's work on eye-contact, summarized in Argyle 1967.

that of about twelve, which does characterize the species in its native state, all members exhibit both physical and psychological withdrawal to a greater degree than may be anticipated for individuals in a customary sized group. Thus we may suspect that if man does have a biological heritage most compatible with life in a relatively closed small social group, then a major function of culture may be to schedule contacts such that their frequency will approximate that which characterized life in the smaller more closed social group of a much earlier stage of biological and cultural evolution.[1]

There may or may not exist historical links between this putative optimal level of effective social contact, and the genesis of social institutions. But irrespective of this, it may be that this 'effective social contact' is the basis of a concealed, subtle and highly variable 'target' for a self-regulating system influencing the size and composition of groups in the day-to-day life of societies. A term like 'effective social contact' begs every question in the book, of course, but since this area of investigation lacks an adequate vocabulary one can only indicate rather crudely the kind of thing one is talking about. The human case naturally is infinitely more complex than the animal, and the chances are that what we are dealing with is not a species-specific 'optimal group size' which can easily be identified in advance, but a situation along the following lines. For any 'communal' event in human social life, no matter how momentary, there is an optimal group size at which the event can efficiently occur—or more simply at which people feel comfortable. This 'optimum', far from being fixed, will be influenced by an almost infinite number of variables. It will itself be an influential factor predominantly in informal, fluid situations rather than formal social gatherings whose size and composition are determined by quite other, institutional requirements. It may be even that an 'optimal' group size is not the significant end-point, but that group size is manipulated along with other variables in the situation (such as the structuring of attention among the participants) to approach yet another kind of 'optimal' state whose nature cannot yet be guessed at.

It will be seen from this that I have no great faith in the rigorous application of a homeostatic model to social life even at the day-to-day level (so far as the regulation of numbers is concerned, at

---

[1] Calhoun 1966. It would be interesting to know whether this is a factor in controlling the spread of disease in 'natural' populations.

least). The reason is a familiar one; one cannot but be suspicious of a claim that groups 'home' cybernetically on to a 'target' in respect of numbers or any other characteristic, when it is impossible to identify the 'target' in advance and hence to check the theory. If we cannot identify the target the argument becomes intolerably *post hoc*, as it tends to be in Wynne-Edwards' thesis. I do not claim that such identification is impossible in principle; but that until we have more idea how to set about it, the proposition that homeostasis in a rigorous sense is an operating principle of human groups must be left in cold storage.

Meanwhile, however, it may be possible to retain in a weaker form the analogy of homeostasis in social life. We could say simply that some evidence (such as that cited above) suggests that in ordinary social life, groups manipulate themselves on certain dimensions—size being one of them—with respect to certain unspecified goals. These 'goals' could be either psychological or social, or both; the difference between this and a 'strict' sense of homeostasis is that here we cannot specify their nature, or even prove their existence. But this fact does not prevent us from looking for possible mechanisms whereby the 'manipulation' could be carried out. And if it is true that 'groups manipulate themselves', then we are entitled to look for such processes operating at the supra-individual level which is legitimately the concern of sociology. We are allowed, that is, to look for 'social facts' governing encounters of the most everyday kind, which may or may not have anything to do with homeostasis in a loose or a tight sense, but are worth investigating in their own right. For example, I mentioned the structuring of attention among members of a group; Chance's recent work on this topic in primates[1] looks as if it could very profitably be extended in investigations of human social life. Goffman has drawn attention[2] to rules which govern the minutiae of social relations, quite as bindingly as their molar aspects are governed by more spectacular, consciously reproducible, regulations. I do not wish to say any more here about this 'human microsociology' and its relation to cultural variations and to corresponding observations in animals; that is the concern of Chapter VII of this book. I merely note here that if there are any homeostatic systems governing human social relations at the everyday level, then Goffman's work on 'situational presence' and how people are admitted

[1] Chance 1967.　　　[2] See e.g. Goffman 1963.

to or excluded from it, does suggest possible mechanisms whereby the size, composition and other variables of face-to-face groups could be systematically manipulated.[1]

It will not have escaped notice that each time we have picked new ground on which to pursue the concept of homeostasis in social life, we have been led to suggestions which do not themselves depend on any homeostatic model for their validity or interest. I reserved judgement on the question of large-scale population homeostasis through social organization, because it has not yet been demonstrated to occur in the human, nor apparently in the animal, case. I rejected the idea of homeostasis as a general source of sociological explanation, because this idea adds nothing to our understanding of (in particular) social control. In Chapter VI I shall approach the problem of 'social control' in animal and human groups by quite a different route. Turning to the field of small-scale, everyday social life, I allowed that homeostatic systems might govern the size, composition and other characteristics of groups, particularly in informal situations, but concluded that it was fruitless even here to apply a homeostatic model of a rigorous biological kind, because in the present state of knowledge the 'fit' of such a model cannot be checked. A far better plan was to find out what variables are important in this micro-structure of social life; to investigate, for example, the concept of 'effective' social contact and its relation to 'actual' contact in different situations. Even the consideration of social homeostasis in a loose sense led straight to the far more interesting question of techniques whereby groups could manipulate themselves, irrespective of whether such manipulations form part of any 'homeostatic' system.

Why then does the idea of homeostasis turn out to be such a comparative dud, after seeming to provide so promising a link between biological and social science (and specifically, between ethology and social anthropology)? Part of the answer may be as follows. A homeostatic model such as Wynne-Edwards' draws together a variety of phenomena by ascribing to them a common function. (Cf. Brown's argument that one can make valid functional statements only within the framework of self-regulating

---

[1] Cf. also Hall's work (1963) on 'proxemic' behaviour, which indicates that there may be a 'grammar' for the structuring of microspace in human encounters.

systems.)[1] Hence on this line of thinking it would tend to be assumed that the significant links between animal and human social life are functional ones, growing out of this and similar functional groupings of data. But such might not be the case. Despite the predominantly functional standpoint of most modern ethologists[2], it seems likely to me that the most interesting connections between animal and human social organization will turn out to be structural rather than functional ones. The questions into which we were led from the discussion of social homeostasis, for example, do seem to be structural questions. At any rate, a structural approach to common elements in human and animal social life is initially sounder, because less question-begging, than an exclusively functional one. If there are functional uniformities as well, they can presumably be filled in at a later stage of investigation, once the basic patterns have been established. This, it seems to me, is the general lesson to be learnt from the 'social homeostasis' discussion. As will be seen in the chapters to follow, this idea of a structural approach in ethology as well as in social anthropology, leads us in a number of interesting directions.

[1] Brown 1963, p. 111.
[2] M. R. A. Chance is an exception to this; he advocates returning to a more 'structural' point of view even within ethology. His approach is discussed in Chapter VIII.

VI

AGGRESSION AND SOCIAL CONTROL

THE idea is not new that human aggressive behaviour can usefully be interpreted in the light of animal studies. For example, in 1916 Trotter engagingly declared:

When I compare German society with the wolf pack, and the feelings, desires and impulses of the individual German with those of the wolf or dog, I am not intending to use a vague analogy but to call attention to a real and gross identity ... The psychical necessity that makes the wolf brave in a massed attack is the same as that which makes the German brave in a massed attack; the psychical necessity which makes the dog submit to the whip of his master and profit by it makes the German soldier submit to the lash of his officer and profit by it.
    ... In studying the mind of England in the spirit of the biological psychologist, it is necessary to keep in mind the society of the bee, just as in studying the German mind it was necessary to keep in mind the society of the wolf ...[1]

The central concern of this chapter is the concept of 'social control' in anthropology, its proper scope and the assumptions which underlie it. I wish to enquire, firstly, whether there is anything in the social organization of animals which can legitimately be called 'social control', and if there is, whether this fact should lead us to suspect that the anthropologists' use of the term 'social control' has been unduly biassed in favour of the exclusively human components of human societies. It may be that the development of an ethological idea of 'social control' would call for a revision or redefinition of the concept of 'social control' in anthropology.

Now it is obvious that in human life many kinds of behaviour are restricted or proscribed by the rules governing a society; and it would be hard to give a universal and *a priori* answer to the question 'What is it that "social control" controls?' But we may reasonably assume that capricious or ungoverned violence, at least

[1] Trotter 1916, pp. 191–2, 203.

among members of a social group, is one of the things which any mechanisms of 'social control' can be expected to minimize. I therefore restrict this discussion to the limited field of 'social control' in relation to aggression, not because there is anything special about aggression, but because the social control of aggression seems likely to be an important instance of 'social control' in human societies, and because the published material on aggression itself is abundant and sophisticated enough to enable us, by this route, to work towards an ethological account of 'social control'.

One way of approaching the problems to be discussed below, is to suppose that the aggressive tendency is an essential component of any complex organization, whether human or animal; that it also creates a fundamental problem, similarly common to all such organizations; that the evolutionary process has 'recognized' this problem and 'made provision' for it to be resolved; and that our job here is to find out what elements of human social life are to be understood by their relation to the mechanisms which control the aggression of aggressive animals. Such an argument would closely parallel the Wynne-Edwards approach to population control, discussed earlier. This picture is part of the truth; and a good part too, as I shall argue below. It is the basis of much recent discussion on the relevance of animal studies to the problem of aggression in human society; discussion which centres round the existence in man of an innate inhibitory mechanism 'designed' to prevent the slaughter of a defeated and submissive adversary. For example Freeman, arguing that the possibility of 'biological' controls on aggression is of enormous interest in the anthropological study of conflict, says:

. . . There is good ethological evidence that in many species gestures of submission do tend to inhibit aggression, and the invention of weapons capable of being used at a distance (which has been a constant trend in the evolution of weapons) is certainly counter to any such natural inhibitory process. Here is a problem which might well be taken up by ethologists and anthropologists alike . . .[1]

But in addition, I should like throughout this chapter to bear in mind the hint that emerged from Chapter v that it may be a mistake to suppose that all the interesting links between human and animal social life are functional ones, based on the classification of material

[1] Freeman 1964, p. 122.

according to the functions it is assumed to serve or to have served. The present chapter, and Chapters VII and VIII, could be read partly as attempts to develop an alternative view that despite the overwhelming functional bias of traditional ethology there is much to be gained from a 'structural' approach (in some sense of the word) to comparisons between animal and human social life. What is implied by 'structure' will, I hope, gradually become clearer in the discussions to follow; and an explicit formulation will be attempted in Chapter IX.

ANTHROPOLOGICAL VIEWS OF 'SOCIAL CONTROL'

It might be misleading to refer at all to a concept of social control in anthropology, since the term appears to have such a variety of senses—were it not, in fact, in such common use. Evidently many social anthropologists feel the need for a concept of 'social control' even though they are by no means agreed on what it means. The *Dictionary of Social Science* distinguishes two clusters of meaning carried by the term 'social control'. The first stresses the fact that the control of individual action performs social functions for the group of which the individual is a member, while the second—which includes doctrines of orthodox Marxism—notes that social means can be used to coerce people, whether to the advantage of society as a whole or to that of a group of individual exploiters. 'Control which is social in its mechanisms may not be social or societal in its functions, . . . and . . . much control which appears to be societal in its functions may actually be serving better the interests of dominant groups.'[1]

But even within the first group of meanings there is precious little uniformity. The anthropological study of 'social control' is commonly associated, or even identified, with that of 'primitive law'. This is implied in Nadel's definition (1952).[1] He 'distinguishes between "self-regulation" and social control, the former being traditional behaviour which needs few social controls because it is related to an "instrumental nexus" and has "value" attached to it, and the latter operating when self-regulation is weakened.' On the other hand a lawyer, Geoffrey Sawer, has[2] rejected the term 'social

---

[1] For all these references see Wolff, Kurt H., Social Control; in Gould & Kolb (ed.) 1964, *Dictionary of the Social Sciences* pp. 650–2.

[2] Sawer 1965, pp. 129–30.

control' altogether as applying to legal systems on the English model, because it is so seldom clear at what points in their lives people are being controlled, and by what means. Park and Burgess (1921)[1] say that 'all social problems turn out finally to be problems of social control', and Gurvitch (1945)[1] defines social control as 'the whole of cultural patterns . . . whereby inclusive society, every particular group, and every participating individual member overcome tensions and conflicts . . . through temporary equilibria and take steps for new creative efforts.' Thus some say that everything is 'social control', others that nothing is, while at least one author defines social control in opposition to an idea of 'self-regulation' which might include the very processes which an ethological comparison would uncover.

In *Crime and Custom in Savage Society* Malinowski does not, I believe, actually use the term 'social control'. Yet it is worth examining his account, in order to gain an idea of what might be understood by 'social control' on a traditional structural/functionalist view. As far as primitive law is concerned, Malinowski is chiefly anxious to emphasize that an ethnography which limits itself to 'central authority, codes, courts and constables' must inevitably distort the picture of social life in any community. His argument, however, is not that behaviour can be controlled at a number of levels besides that of overt, public, 'legal' institutions, but rather that evasions of the law are common, and are themselves frequently tolerated and even partly institutionalized.

When the native is asked what he would do in such-and-such a case, he answers what he *should* do; he lays down the pattern of best possible conduct. When he acts as informant to a field-anthropologist, it costs him nothing to retail the Ideal of the law. His sentiments, his propensities, his bias, his self-indulgences as well as tolerance of others' lapses, he reserves for his behaviour in real life . . . The other side, the natural, impulsive code of conduct , the evasions, the compromises and non-legal usages are revealed only to the field-worker, who . . . lives at such close quarters with his 'material' as to understand not only their language and their statements, but also the hidden motives of behaviour and the hardly ever formulated spontaneous line of conduct.[2]

---

[1] For all these references see Wolff, Kurt H., Social Control; in Gould & Kolb (ed.) 1964, *Dictionary of the Social Sciences* pp. 650-2.

[2] Malinowski 1926, pp. 120–21.

This 'spontaneous line of conduct' plays a multiple rôle in Malinowski's theory. That it is not implacably opposed to law and order is implied by his remark that the savage's 'observance of the rules of law under normal conditions . . . is not enforced by any wholesale motive like fear of punishment, or a general submission to all tradition, but by very complex psychological and social inducements.'[1] But elsewhere he expresses more strongly the view that the inborn nature of man is the raw material for social control, nothing more:

The fundamental function of law is to curb certain natural propensities, to hem in and control human instincts and to impose a non-spontaneous compulsory behaviour—in other words, to secure a type of co-operation which is based on mutual concessions and sacrifices for a common end. A new force, different from the innate, spontaneous endowment must be present to perform this task.[2]

It would be inaccurate, however, to claim that Malinowski sees no middle ground between legal institutions and self-interested evasions of them. He does envisage social control in terms of a continuum of some kind:

. . . Besides the main division between quasi-civil and quasi-criminal . . . a distinction must be made between the various grades of law which can be arranged into a hierarchy from the statutes of main legitimate law, through legally tolerated usages down to evasions and traditional methods of flouting the law.[3]

But his account implies that as we move down the hierarchy, behaviour becomes progressively de-controlled; actions and habits which flout the law are 'under control' only to the extent that they are themselves tacitly recognized as institutions. There is no room in the Malinowskian picture for the possibility that the 'spontaneous line of conduct', far from being just a diffuse and unitary 'human nature', may itself have multiple strands; that it may itself embody controls on behaviour no less real and interesting than those of 'codes, courts, and constables'—and, moreover, no less 'social'. This possibility is thrown wide open, I shall argue below, if we accept that an ethological definition of 'social control' could have consequences at a human societal level.

[1] ibid., pp. 14–15.   [2] ibid., p. 64.   [3] ibid., p. 124.

'SOCIAL CONTROL' IN ANIMALS

(a) *The control of fighting in animals*

It would be a lengthy task to try to evaluate all the claims and controversies which surround the concept of aggression in ethology and psychology. There is more than one approach to this topic. The 'psychological' school (to use a very rough label) derives its strongest influence from the work of Dollard and his associates,[1] who '. . . conceive aggression, not as an inherent genetically given quantum of energy seeking expression but rather as a by-product of frustration, initially the invariable response to it.'[2] The post-Darwinian biologists on the other hand have viewed aggressive behaviour in a wider context of survival and selection pressure. Aggression thus becomes one of the fundamental instruments for the organization of social life in many species; hence aggressive potential, and the situations which evoke it, are part of the genetic equipment of these species. The biological attitude to aggression finds an unexpected ally in Freud, whose 'dual instinct theory . . . conceives the individual as genetically endowed with a given amount or quantum of energy directed towards destructiveness in the widest sense and which must inevitably be expressed in some form or other.'[3] Since this discussion is about the implications of the 'biological' view of aggression, it is this which I propose to adopt.

The existence of aggression in many species as an 'instinctive' tendency, has at least two kinds of consequence. Firstly there is the evolution of mechanisms 'designed' to restrict the number of situations in which intra-specific violence can occur, and to limit its effects; and secondly there is the possibility that elements of social life are phylogenetically dependent on this same 'controlled' aggressiveness. Lorenz's *On Aggression* is chiefly an exposition of the view that the bond of personal attachment where it exists in animals is the evolutionary consequence of the ritualized redirection of an aggressive impulse which is itself of strong survival value to the species. Hence '. . . love is the complement of group aggressiveness. Love between mates of a pair, friendship between members of a group are most strikingly developed in species in which the pair or the group have to be aggressive against other pairs

---

[1] See e.g. Dollard et al. 1939, *Frustration and Aggression*, (New Haven, Yale University Press.)

[2] Hill 1964.   [3] ibid.

or groups.'[1] But we are principally concerned here with the first problem mentioned above: by what means is overt fighting in animals brought under control?

It is generally acknowledged nowadays that overt fighting among members of a species is rare, and is considerably rarer in the wild than in captivity. The point is often made with the implied inference that fighting is rare 'because' it is minimized by behavioural controls: '. . . an important part of animal behaviour, at least in the mammals, is directed towards avoiding intraspecific fighting. The weapons are potentially so dangerous that fighting is ritualized into display, threat and submission or appeasement, so that fights are generally no more than trials of strength followed by disengagement and rapid withdrawal by the weaker . . .'[2]

Controls on fighting or bloodshed in animals are not always 'social' in any real sense. They may consist, for example, of 'defence movements so well adapted to the species-specific form of attack that the latter is almost invariably parried'—or even of 'merely passive armour.'[3] But it seems that there do exist controls on animal aggression which are 'social' in the sense that they operate through characteristics of the social behaviour of the species in question. The 'social controls' on aggression which have been most intensively studied by ethologists fall into two main groups. (Needless to say these groups are not mutually exclusive; they often coincide in observed situations.) On the one hand we find control exercised through characteristics of the social organization of the species—this could be termed 'structural control'. On the other, bloodshed is apparently minimized by modifications in the technique of fighting itself; that is, by the development of 'ritualized' gestures of various kinds as part of the innate behavioural equipment of the species. Each of these topics has been a central concern of ethologists for many years; they are very fully explored in the literature, and I shall discuss them in no more detail here than is necessary before considering what is implied by 'social control' in ethology.

To begin with what looks like the 'structural' control of aggression, it appears that simple avoidance is often sufficient to keep the peace, for example among solitary mammals. Free-living cats deposit scent-marks along their pathways, but according to

---

[1] Tinbergen 1966.   [2] Harrison Matthews 1964.
[3] Lorenz 1964.

Leyhausen[1] there is no evidence that these marks actually intimidate other individuals. Instead, one of their functions may be '. . . to avoid unexpected encounters and sudden clashes, another [function] to tell who is ahead on the road and how far, and whether he can be met if required.' Of course it is not certain that the leaving of scent marks has anything to do with 'social control'; one can only argue backwards from the fact that social breakdown and destructive fighting occur when cats are prevented from maintaining their characteristic social distances. Clearly there is a need for more experimental studies in this area.

For expositions of the view that dominance and territorial systems have as one of their consequences the control of aggression, see for example Scott[2] and Etkin.[3] Etkin's second paper is a particularly thorough-going survey of different types of social organizations, relating the characteristic behaviour of animal groups to environmental pressures such as the danger from predators. He makes the point that where (as in wolves) subsistence depends on co-operative hunting, competitive fighting is kept under control by a 'mild' form of dominance which does not involve the exclusion of young males from the group, as in macaques. Hence 'the pack-hunting ecology would be expected to shift the mating system from the macaque type toward the integrated family with the elimination of mating competition among family members' and '. . . we should look more to the wolf than to the macaque as a basic model for understanding protocultural man.'[4] Such a view could well be taken into account in formulating a theory of the origins of incest taboos and exogamy.[5]

Often aggression is visibly controlled by the action of dominant animals in suppressing fighting among their subordinates.[6] Hediger describes the annual 'cow fights' in the Val d'Anniviers of the Wallis canton of Switzerland, and goes on: 'The queen is usually adorned with a particularly fine cow bell. It is not a fact that she always leads the herd when it moves on but she invariably uses her full authority . . . generally separating fighting members, as other alpha animals do.'[7]

Occasionally the boot is on the other foot. Hall[8] reports groups of female baboons ganging up to threaten a dominant male which

[1] Leyhausen 1965.   [2] Scott 1962.   [3] Etkin 1964 and 1964a.
[4] ibid. 1964.   [5] Cf. Fox 1967a, pp. 64–5.
[6] Hall 1963.   [7] Hediger 1955, p. 73.   [8] Hall 1962.

was attacking another female, 'with the regular effect of making the male withdraw.' Hall himself stresses the stability of dominance relationships as a prime factor in keeping fighting to a minimum, the evidence being a report from Uganda that serious fighting regularly broke out in baboons after the shooting of a large male.[1] It certainly seems true that species which have strong dominance hierarchies are also equipped to learn dominance relationships very quickly and to retain them for long periods with minimal reinforcement.

Leyhausen's[2] work on cats leads one to suspect that from the point of view of 'social control' dominance and possibly territory may represent more sophisticated versions of avoidance. Ranking may be a technique for keeping down direct encounters between individuals (cf. Chapter v, p. 56)—indeed, subordinate rank is often expressed and acknowledged by avoiding the dominant animal or moving out of its way.[3] This might explain why a hierarchical organization tends to arise, abnormally, when space has run out. Thus this aspect of 'social control' may turn out in the end to be a question of physical and social distances.

The other way in which violence is said to be controlled is through modifications in the technique of fighting; i.e. through 'ritualization' of part or all of the procedure of a fight. The topic of ritualization and its place in animal and human social life clearly merits a separate study, drawing together threads from anthropology, ethology, clinical psychology and psychiatry—not to mention literature, art and history. I do not propose to embark on this huge topic here, partly because such a study has already been attempted,[4] and partly because, as I said in Chapter III (p. 34), the Huxley symposium made surprisingly little progress towards integrating the biological and sociological approaches to 'ritualization' and 'ritual'. In passing, however, I would like to note two ethological formulations concerning 'ritualization' which promise to be helpful in an anthropological account of ritual. The first is Morris's concept of 'typical intensity', which points the way to an identification of the ritualized act in terms of the elimination of signal ambiguity by 'the development of a frequency–intensity relationship in which very great changes in the frequency of a response are only accompanied by very small changes in its form.'[5]

[1] ibid.   [2] Leyhausen 1965.   [3] See e.g. Simonds 1965 and Jay 1965.
[4] Huxley (ed.) 1966.   [5] Morris 1957.

This clearly fits with the 'measured' quality typical of human ceremonious behaviour. The second is the 'emancipation' of the ritualized act from its 'primary' motivation or motivational conflict, whereby it is said to acquire properties and releasing mechanisms similar to those of an independent drive.[1] This concept of 'emancipation' will become important when we consider greeting ceremonies in Chapter VII.

But apart from the general problem of developing a concept of 'ritualization' to span both animal and human social organizations, 'ritualized' gestures are claimed to play a crucial rôle in controlling aggression in animals. They are said to achieve this by allowing a dispute to be setted without violence, or, if fighting occurs, by stopping it before serious damage is done to the loser.[2] Thus 'threat' and 'submission' are opposite sides of the same coin, although the use of such terms begs the question a little. Such gestures do seem well-designed to exhibit any clear difference in fighting potential between contestants while giving the weaker animal a chance to withdraw in time. This does not always happen in quite the way one would expect; there is at least a sharp surface analogy between the following two tales, which are worth quoting at length. It would not be wrong, I think, to speak of 'confrontation' in both cases:

Two noble lords, Chin and Ch'in, face one another encamped. The two armies are ranged and do not fight. At night a messenger from Ch'in comes to warn Chin to get ready: 'There is no lack of warriors in the two armies! Tomorrow I engage you to meet us!' But the people of Chin notice that the messenger has an unsteady gaze and that his voice has no assurance. Ch'in is beaten beforehand. 'The Ch'in army is afraid of us! It will take to flight! Let us hem them in against the river! Certainly we will beat them!' Yet the Chin army does not move, and the enemy can decamp in peace. It has sufficed for someone to say, 'It is inhuman not to gather up the dead and wounded! It is cowardly not to wait for the time arranged, or to press upon the enemy in a dangerous passage.' So Chin's army keeps quiet and leaves the enemy to draw off in peace.[3]

That not-being-impressed makes a deep impression is a very general principle . . . In the wonderful ritual fights of the fence lizard, each of the rivals first holds his heavily armoured head in an attitude of self-

---

[1] See e.g. Hinde and Tinbergen 1958; Blest 1961; Lorenz 1966a.
[2] See e.g. Harrison Matthews 1964; Lorenz 1964.
[3] Huizinga 1949, p. 97, citing Granet's *Chinese Civilization.*

display towards the other, until one seizes the other. After a short wrestling match, he lets go and waits till the other in his turn seizes him . . . Now in lizards, as in many other 'cold-blooded' animals, smaller individuals 'get going' quicker than larger ones . . . This means that in the ritual fight of the fence lizard, with a certain degree of regularity the smaller of the two fighters is the first to seize the other by the back of the head and pull him to and fro. When there is much difference in size, it may happen that the smaller one, having let go, does not await the return bite of the larger one, but at once performs the submissive gesture . . . and then flees. He has noticed from the purely passive resistance that his adversary is superior.[1]

This reminds Lorenz not of Chinese military lore, but of a sequence from a Chaplin film.

An important point in relation to this kind of 'social control' of aggression is that in animals there is no sharp division between 'ritualized' and 'real' combat, which also has its ritual elements.[2] The 'ritual' component of animal fights is seen in the stereotyped and predictable way in which they characteristically end. Under 'natural' conditions the loser is generally able either to break away and flee or to adopt an 'appeasement' posture which is said to inhibit further attack.[3] It used to be said[4] that the appeasing element of these displays was the offering of a vulnerable part of the body to the aggressor; nowadays more stress is placed on the fact that the 'submissive' gesture tends to be the 'natural opposite' of the threat displays of the species, and on its character as a de- or re-motivating agent.[5] If this principle of the 'natural opposite' holds in the animal's perception of the situation as well as the observer's, then we are approaching the notion of a 'symbolic' use of space by animals.

Incidentally, this shading into one another of 'ritualized' and 'real' combat may have had important consequences for the development of human fighting techniques; there is some evidence

[1] Lorenz 1966, pp. 107–8.
[2] See e.g. Harrison Matthews 1964.
[3] Chance (1962) has recently suggested that these two moves represent alternative pathways of response available to the animal; and has discussed the factors which may determine its choice.
[4] e.g. by Lorenz in *King Solomon's Ring* (1952).
[5] See Morris 1964; comment in Carthy & Ebling (eds), p. 37; and Chance 1962. But as I have said the relation of 'submissive' gestures such as pseudo-infantile or pseudo-sexual displays to their 'primary' motivation, is not always clear-cut.

(to be discussed later) that the use of objects in intimidation displays by primates may merge into the evolution of the weapon.[1]

(b) *The idea of 'social control' in ethology*

I have cited a number of instances of what might be called the social control of aggression in animals. Is it possible now to attach a meaning to the term 'social control' in ethology, either in relation to aggression or more generally? A simple view of the social control of aggression would involve the assumption that a problem is 'initially' presented by the 'prior' existence of a tendency to destructive violence, which 'requires' to be brought under control. Such a view would imply that without controls there would be widespread slaughter in aggressive species, and therefore that removal or breakdown of the controls would expose the nature of 'primitive' expression of the aggressive impulse. This view would be only partly accurate, although it has been tacitly followed by me so far. Thus I have cited some of the arguments which claim that the potential for fighting can be explained by the multiple part it plays in the adaptation of aggressive species to their total life conditions, but that this readiness to fight is itself potentially dangerous to the species, and so is hedged around with controls of various kinds, many of them social in character. It is inevitable that for the purpose of discussion one divides a subject up and treats topics one by one; but this should not be allowed to obscure the fact that patterns of behaviour, like social institutions, are essentially interrelated and structured within a total system. To take a 'single' behavioural system and study it in isolation is a potentially misleading approach to behaviour as a whole. For example it is puzzling to find Etkin[2] arguing that dominance and territory are important agents for the control of aggression in animals, while Davis in the same volume[3] maintains that 'the major function of aggressive behaviour is to determine and maintain rank or territory.' This paradox, I think, illustrates not the falsity of either position but the fact that to take behavioural systems 'in series' in this way is a basically artificial procedure. So what we want to know now is how far the controls on aggressive behaviour enumerated above are separable from what they control, either conceptually or in operation.

[1] See Kortlandt and Kooij 1963.
[2] Etkin 1964.   [3] Davis 1964.

One can certainly find support in the literature for a view that 'aggression' in animals is distinguishable from 'social control' in the sense of predating it in evolutionary time. For example, Lorenz believes that 'there may be other independent ways in which bond behaviour has evolved, but wherever it did, it seems to have done so as a means of controlling aggression, that is to say on the basis of aggressive behaviour pre-existing.'[1]

Again, there is some evidence—experimental in the broad sense of the deliberate creation of non-natural situations—on what 'uncontrolled' aggression would look like. This comes from at least two sources, corresponding to the two broad divisions into which I have placed the methods of controlling aggression in animals—namely, control achieved through the structural properties of a social organization and control operating through components of innately determined techniques of fighting. Firstly, if fighting is a distance-increasing agent producing dispersal which in turn acts as a check on violence, then any sabotage of this reciprocal system would be expected to result, by a positive feedback, in the kind of violent social breakdown reported by many writers.[2] Secondly, it is apparently possible to interfere with the ritualized components of fighting. Scott and his associates trained mice to be 'fighters' after which the mice would attack an adversary without the customary preliminaries:

When mice fight, their emotional reactions consist chiefly of fluffing the hair and rattling the tail. When two male mice are put together, we often see them approaching each other cautiously, fluffing their hair and shaking their tails, and then suddenly begin to fight. However, if we train a mouse to fight with a series of easy victories, he never shows this emotional behaviour but leaps upon his next victim in a fraction of a second.[3]

Scott's conclusion is that 'emotional behaviour is not a necessary part of fighting'. On the contrary, the point is that these displays (which may be 'emotional' in the sense of being conflict-generated) are an integral part of fighting, but can be by-passed by training. All this amounts to saying that the social controls on aggression in animals can be made to break down, by preventing avoidance in its

[1] Lorenz 1964.
[2] For a selection of references on this point see Harrison Matthews 1964.
[3] Scott 1958, p. 59.

various forms or by interfering with the ritualized actions which regularly accompany fighting and are assumed often to replace it.[1]

One can, then, go some way towards exposing the nature of 'primitive' aggression in animals when controls have broken down; and one can find instances of fighting being, apparently, dramatically checked by an 'appeasement' gesture or by an exercise of dominance from a third party. But it does not follow that the controls should be thought of as 'sitting on' primitive aggression in the way that the Malinowskian picture of social control places legal or quasi-legal processes fairly and squarely on top of the innate law-breaking tendencies of man. In the case of animal aggression and the control of it, the processes concerned are essentially intertwined and dependent on one another even if they can be forced apart by crude experimental hatchet-work. Scott's mistake (in the passage quoted above) is that he ignores this fact. The idea of a tendency to fight which must be constantly held in and restrained by 'social controls', is something of an artifact. On the one hand, we have the aggressive tendency contributing to a total social structure, which in turn governs behaviour in such a way as to minimize violence among conspecifics. On the other hand, most animal fights are themselves highly controlled affairs, control being exercised through 'ritualized' components at almost every point in the fighting sequence. This can be admitted, I think, even though there is no agreement on the precise meaning of 'ritualization'. So in an ethological definition of 'social control', one would want to stress the 'balanced' quality of social organization where it exists in animals, and the importance of structured and limited aggressiveness in achieving this under normal conditions. Hall writes, for example, of baboons and macaques: 'The overall picture of group organization in these animals is of a sensitive balancing of forces, the balance being achieved by the social learning of individuals in the group from time of birth to adulthood, so that infringements of the group norm are rare.'[2]

Chance[3] argues from a wide range of examples that 'cut-off' acts and postures, which 'reduce the predominant aversive drive,

[1] Barnett & Evans have recently questioned these assumptions about the function of ritualized aggression in small mammals, and have suggested that a 'threatening' display may have the effect of increasing rather than diminishing the likelihood of a fight. See Barnett & Evans 1965. This point will be raised again in connection with ritual in human fighting.

[2] Hall 1964.   [3] Chance 1962.

whether of flight or aggression', preserve a balance in social life by controlling aggression while allowing social animals to remain together. Chance's article and his concept of 'cut-off' suggest further developments of the idea that fighting is often controlled by subtle forms of avoidance. Leyhausen has a particularly vivid picture of the quasi-political organization of a neighbourhood of cats, where all things are relative and the various peacekeeping 'institutions' themselves have limits set to them by other factors. In the following, for example, we are already a good way from the crude statement that 'dominance hierarchies control aggression'— and are approaching the kind of account which a social anthropologist might find relevant to his field. In Leyhausen's cats, it seems, the logic of the social structure ensures that all incentives are against fighting:

The whole social system . . . [of cats] . . . seems . . . designed to ensure that the greatest possible number of strong and healthy males has an almost equal chance of reproduction, rather than to favour exclusively a single dominating individual . . . For what I rather poetically described above as the 'brotherhood' is in fact nothing mythical, but rests on a very real balance of power, risks and deterrents. It can be formed only if there are several males of almost equal strength, so that victories and defeats are decided by a narrow margin and it might cost a higher ranking male his superiority if he provoked an inferior so far as to make him actually fight.[1]

AGGRESSION AND HUMAN SOCIETY

(a) *Aggressiveness in man*

Is man aggressive in the sense that many animals are? In other words, is *Homo sapiens* one of the species whose basic social organization rests partly on the inbuilt aggressive tendency in individuals? A more interesting question is: can human aggressiveness be 'taken for granted' by the social scientist much as, at a certain level, the actions involved in eating are taken for granted? Or is it as complex in itself as I have tried to show animal aggressiveness to be, itself requiring a thorough analysis before we can understand the human institutions which surround it?

Questions about human aggression are apt to be misleadingly put. I suspect that Lorenz leads himself astray by taking too simple an initial view of the problem, as where he maintains that 'human

[1] Leyhausen 1965. The terms 'political' and 'institution' are mine, not his.

behaviour, and particularly human social behaviour, far from being determined by reason and cultural tradition alone, is still subject to all the laws prevailing in all phylogenetically adapted instinctive behaviour.'[1] All?—one wants to ask. Lorenz holds that an aggressive impulse, bred into man perhaps by intra-specific selection pressures which created the 'warrior virtues' as cultural values, is in its 'original' form (somehow) a mainspring of human action in contemporary society. This may be so, but to demonstrate the truth of the hypothesis is surely not as simple a matter as Lorenz seems to think. If it is difficult to find in animals cases of 'primal' aggression occurring independently of the social processes which channel it, it is even more doubtful to look for examples of human aggressiveness divorced (except perhaps in the youngest children) from its societal realizations. This is a subaspect of the problem I raised in Chapter IV (p. 52)—whether one could write an ethogram of the human species without this amounting to a catalogue of all human action and experience.

In the human even more than the animal case, there is a clear need to analyse the various concepts connected with violent behaviour. We must make an initial distinction between 'aggression', 'fighting', 'killing' and 'warfare', however these may turn out to be interconnected. On this view, aggression in human beings is something of a theoretical construct—rather more so than is aggression in animals. The connection with fighting is not so obvious, because of the subtle forms in which human aggression can be expressed—e.g. in verbal and symbolic behaviour. Nor can we be quite so certain of a clear physiological basis for human aggression, because of the difficulties of collecting evidence. So we must be a little wary of claiming that human beings are 'innately' aggressive in the way that wolves or baboons—or even breeding male sticklebacks—are; and this in spite of the strong circumstantial evidence furnished by the broad functional uniformities of the mammalian central nervous system, by apparently spontaneous fighting among children, and by human evolutionary history if Lorenz is right. Thus the fact that the criteria for recognizing human aggression are different from the animal case and in many respects unique, presents us with a difficulty in isolating the problem. For this discussion does require some concept of 'aggressive' fighting among men (or more accurately, of 'aggressive'

[1] Lorenz 1966, p. 204.

violence, since it might be thought that fighting presupposes aggression) to which ethological interpretations might apply. Not all violence, nor even all intra-specific violence, in human beings is directly aggressive. For example, the very term 'head-hunting' suggests that the violent act involved is more akin to predation than to aggression in animals, although it may of course serve wider aggressive ends:

An aspect of the mentality of people addicted to such institutionalized forms of violence as head-hunting or human sacrifice is the absence of any deep emotional involvement in acts of wounding or killing . . . The head-hunter . . . who seeks a victim because he wants to gain the status and privileges of a warrior or because his village or men's house requires a head for ritual purposes, may have no personal animosity vis-à-vis the intended victim . . . Konyak Nagas were certainly not inspired by any ill-feeling against the slaves they bought in order to obtain heads without running the risks of raiding, and I remember well how an elderly Konyak expressed pity for a boy he and his fellow-clansmen had bought with the express purpose of cutting off his head . . . In . . . these cases killing is an action undertaken to achieve specific results but not motivated by fury or personal feelings of hatred.[1]

Perhaps the best we can do is to stipulate rather loosely that what we are talking about is violence, or its substitutes, motivated by feelings of aggression which a psychiatrist or an ordinary person would recognize. One does not want to get bogged down in mental behaviourism. Despite the philosophical difficulty of comparing human and animal aggression where the criteria of identification are different, the strongest justification for admitting a concept of human aggressiveness to sociology if not to biology is the natural way in which 'aggression' fits into people's interpretations of one another's actions.

The idea of aggression in human beings, then, is in this context distinct from those of fighting, killing and warfare (despite the frequent use of 'aggression' in the vocabulary of international politics, to equal 'armed attack'). This is important, because it can be argued that while 'aggression' and its linkages with ethology can probably account for fighting between one person and another, quite different factors are involved in regular intra-specific killing and in warfare, both of which appear to be almost exclusively human habits. As far as the former of these is concerned, many

[1] Von Fürer-Haimendorf 1967, pp. 113–14.

writers have argued that human beings are unique among animals in their murderous behaviour towards conspecifics.[1] The fact that human far more than animal fights are apt to end in serious injury or death of the losing party, is often said to be a simple result of the human use of weapons. It is commonly pointed out[2] that most weapons act at a distance, and that they act more randomly as well as more lethally than an assault with teeth or fists. Each of these factors, the argument goes, would tend to sabotage any killing inhibition 'designed' to be evoked by the defeated adversary. Lorenz has a slightly different view, maintaining that

One can only deplore the fact that man has definitely not got a carnivorous mentality! All his trouble arises from his being a basically harmless, omnivorous creature, lacking in natural weapons with which to kill big prey, and therefore, also devoid of the built-in safety devices which prevent 'professional' carnivores from abusing their killing power to destroy fellow-members of their own species.[3]

He is not, however, entirely consistent on this point, claiming on the same page that

In human evolution, no inhibitory mechanisms preventing sudden manslaughter were necessary, because quick killing was impossible anyhow; the potential victim had plenty of opportunity to elicit the pity of the aggressor by submissive gestures and appeasing attitudes.[4]

All this is true and applies to human fighting which is aggressively motivated. But as I said above, not all human violence is aggressive in a straightforward way. It is possible that what weapons quite often do is not to release the aggressive impulse from the built-in controls on it but rather to divorce aggression in all its controlled complexity from fighting altogether. This is more likely to happen in large- than in small-scale combat, and becomes important, as I shall show, when one looks at the connection between aggression and warfare. In addition, one must recognize the difference which weapons make to the sheer strategy of fighting. It becomes quite simply the best policy to kill one's enemy, despite any built-in reluctance to do so. The point is well made by Andreski:

Fisticuffs usually end with thrashings or the flight of the beaten; killing need not be a by-product of fighting, although it may follow it and be

[1] See e.g. Andreski 1964, Durbin & Bowlby 1939, Freeman 1964.
[2] See e.g. Rifkin 1963.   [3] Lorenz 1966, p. 207.
[4] ibid.

done on purpose. Furthermore, in such a situation a victor does not have to fear the vengeance of the weaker opponent. But this is not so if weapons are used, because then he who stabs or shoots first wins, and under such circumstances it is safest to kill one's enemies.[1]

So despite the unique prevalence of killing in human violence, it is worthwhile to compare aggressive fighting in animals and men, if only to discover at what points aggression and social control in an ethological sense enter into lethal violence between men, and what difference weapon technology contributes. Andreski argues that 'the natural propensities of man do not account for the systematic killing in which mankind indulges, because this practice is at variance with what goes on among other mammals.' This is at once an assertion of strong links between human and animal behaviour, and a denial of their adequacy for the explanation of human violence. The view I am putting forward would, paradoxically, be doubtful about these 'natural propensities of man' because of the strong evidence that man's genetic programming renders him inseparable from *a* culture and *a* technology.[2] On the other hand, I maintain that although killing in fighting and the use of weapons may be uniquely human (or nearly so) a full account of the connections between them demands a comparative study of aggressive fighting in different species, and especially of its controlled and 'ritualized' components. This is not to deny that killing is frequently dictated by quite other, specifically human (such as political or economic) motives. (In these cases, it is interesting that any built-in controls which would 'normally' prevent such action are characteristically blocked, often ritually so; cf. the condemned man's hood. It is said that a large ration of drink was issued beforehand to SS men ordered to carry out massacres of civilians in occupied countries, and there is evidence that alcohol can effectively de-inhibit violence.)

An even more obvious problem than the question of killing is the relation of human aggressiveness to organized warfare at the level of societies, and this has received correspondingly more attention in the literature. Most writers recognize that the issue is complex, although one occasionally comes across a naïve view such as Durbin and Bowlby's, that: '. . . the simplest and most general causes of war are only to be found in the causes of fighting, just as

---

[1] Andreski 1964.   [2] See Geertz 1964.

the simplest and most general causes of falling downstairs are to be found in the causes of falling down.'[1]

But the questions preoccupying most current writers on the subject of aggression and warfare, and the lack of an answer to them, have been accurately summarized by Carthy and Ebling:

Is human aggression innate? The current psychiatric evidence seems almost unequivocal; aggression is not merely a response to frustration, it is a deep-seated, universal drive. But is this part of the aetiology of war, and can the aggression of states in any sense be equated with the aggression of individuals? Agreement on the answer to this problem is not reached; indeed the very question appears to challenge the disciplinary frontiers of the sociologist and historian.[2]

Benedict believes that warfare and aggression are not to be identified with each other in any sense. 'Warfare is not the expression of the instinct of pugnacity. Man's pugnacity is so small a hint in the human equipment that it may not be given any expression in intertribal relations.'[3] Burton denies any strong connection between aggression on the part of individuals and of nation-states, and castigates 'the intellectual in society' for 'encouraging every state to have an expectation of aggression, even though there is no discernible enemy.'[4] Kalmus writes 'That wars between states cannot be simply explained as a consequence of aggressive behaviour . . . can be readily conceded, though aggressive acts of individuals or small groups, such as political assassinations, have on several occasions precipitated major wars and group hostility seems to be a regular concomitant of war.'[5]

Lorenz's view of the connection between aggression as an innate human endowment, and warfare on an organized scale, is not entirely clear. In *On Aggression* he seems to regard what he calls 'militant enthusiasm' (which can be 'plugged in' to all manner of political goals) as a kind of mediating factor linking the two, but we are given no clearer exposition of this than '. . . militant enthusiasm is a specialized form of communal aggression, clearly distinct from and yet functionally related to the more primitive forms of petty individual aggression.'[6] Yet it is precisely this link which is most necessary to Lorenz's whole argument about the

---

[1] Durbin and Bowlby 1939, p. 3.
[2] Carthy and Ebling in Carthy & Ebling (eds) 1964, p. 3.
[3] Benedict 1934, p. 32.   [4] Burton 1964.
[5] Kalmus 1965.   [6] Lorenz 1966, p. 231.

problems facing civilizations today. Lorenz underestimates the difficulties of relating human aggressiveness to warfare in its modern forms. This shows up, I believe, in his formula for averting social disintegration and war. The road to self-knowledge, according to Lorenz, lies through (a) ethological understanding of how aggression can be re-directed; (b) psycho-analytical study of 'sublimation'; (c) the promotion of friendship between members of opposing ideologies; (d) the 'responsible channelling of militant enthusiasm.'[1] In connection with (a), (b), and (d) one may mention Storr's suggestion[2] that the space race is essentially a ritualization of the cold war.

Lorenz's view of aggression certainly goes some way towards accounting for the prevalence of killing in human fighting, as I discussed above, in terms of the by-passing of an innate 'killing inhibition'. His suggestions on how we can diminish our readiness to fight, are no doubt helpful. But his argument also leads one to realize that much modern warfare is controlled and executed on a totally un-aggressive basis, given, for example, the use of remote-control weapons and the necessity for commanders to be detached from the field of battle. Much of the peril of modern warfare arises not because 'naked aggression' is let loose upon the enemy, but because the human aggressive impulse and the controls it carries within it often do not enter into the waging of war at the points where restraint might be possible. In the present state of knowledge it is difficult to say who would be qualified to decide precisely how aggression, in an ethological sense, enters into warfare. But in *On Aggression* Lorenz has missed the problem completely. Elsewhere, it is true, he repudiates a simple view that aggression and warfare are to be identified in any crude way: 'I do not deny that governments may cause wars without being motivated by anything comparable to the instinctive drive of intraspecific aggression ... But the point is, no politician could ever make men really fight, if it were not for very archaic, instinctive reactions of the crowd on which to play.'[3] This may be contrasted with Andreski's view, which makes no distinction between motivations to make war and motivations to fight: 'if human beings were ... endowed with an innate proclivity for war, it would not be necessary to indoctrinate them with warlike virtues.'[4]

[1] ibid., p. 239.   [2] Storr 1964.
[3] Lorenz 1964 (in 'discussion'), pp. 155-9.   [4] Andreski 1964.

The problem of relating human aggression to human warfare boils down to a confusion about the 'level' of individual or social organization at which the concept of 'aggression' properly applies. I have no solution to offer, but I believe that one is to be looked for along the following lines: I have tried to suggest that 'aggression' in animals is as much a structural concept as it is a functional one. The aggressive tendency is itself structured; this is part of what is meant by saying that fighting is full of 'ritualized' elements. It contributes to an internal motivational structure in the animal and to an external social structure. It is, indeed, a 'social fact', or part of one, for many animals. There is no reason to deny that much of this is true of human aggressiveness. But since human societies are conspicuously built around verbal and symbolic action in the broadest possible senses of these terms, it is to be expected that processes which have their roots in the biology of *Homo sapiens* will recur repeatedly at a number of 'meta-levels' in human social life. These processes not only 'work', as in non-human animals; they are 'used' and 'mentioned' (in something like the logical sense) over and over again. One might say loosely that much of human social action utilizes extended metaphors on systems which in their basic form are the concern of ethology (but are no less 'social' for being so). This may be true of other behavioural systems as well as those surrounding aggression; it may for example lie at the root of the relation between ritualization and ritual (but see Chapter IV, p. 48). It would be wrong, therefore, to mark off a set of human activities and say: 'This much we biologically inherit; the rest is culture'— and if this is what Hampshire means by the following remark, then his view must be rejected: 'One would accept in general about human behaviour that it must be a genetic inheritance with a cultural layer on top, and similarly for ritual behaviours of various kinds.'[1]

We have here a hint of one way in which the content of ethology may be expected to prove useful in understanding human societies, as well as a rebuttal of the accusation that one is 'reducing' human society to biology. As far as the immediate problem is concerned, the moral is that in order to account for collective combat in the human context we need not only an answer to the question 'is man aggressive?' (whatever this means); and not only an explanation of the political, economic and other factors bound up with organized

[1] Hampshire 1968.

warfare, but also an understanding of how aggression and the idea of aggression and the language of aggression, are socially perceived and manipulated at every point.

(b) *Control of human aggression*

The last subsection was concerned with the place of aggression, as an ethologist would understand it, in a sociological account of fighting, killing and warfare in human societies. Whatever may be the final solution to this problem, there remains a further question: whether the idea of 'social control' as it applies to animal aggression is of any significance in the human case. It is worth bearing in mind once more the distinction I made earlier, between control which is brought about through the logic of a social structure and control which arises through built-in components that regularize fighting behaviour. But it is becoming clear that it was misleading to label the former 'structural' control as if the latter were something different. For we are being led to see that 'ritualized' fighting is in some sense 'structured' fighting, and to say that something is structured is very close to saying that it is controlled. What the distinction does reflect is the prevailing assumption that the important links between animal and human social life are functional ones—for it is much easier to apply functional explanations to the 'ritualized' components of fighting than to the other kind of 'social control'. One can easily describe the study of these built-in regularities in animal and human fighting behaviour as a search for 'instincts' common to animals and men which are 'designed to' achieve social control. On the other hand, a functional approach to the control of aggression through social structure—e.g. through dominance and territoriality—has an obviously less happy outcome, as we saw earlier in this chapter (p. 83) where it appeared that functional explanations of aggression and dominance or aggression and territory can only be given in a circular way. A functional account of the 'ritualized' elements of fighting in animals and men is not, however, ruled out; as I said in the first section of this chapter such an account would contain a good deal of truth. The point is that to reveal the functional status of such elements is not to exclude their structured and structuring properties from the explanation of social control. I shall accordingly consider the rôle of 'ritualized' acts and gestures in human fighting. But first something must be said about the human versions of the other kind of social control on aggression, that achieved through the more obviously structural characteristics of a social organization.

One would expect 'simple avoidance' to have its human counterpart, at any rate in the forestalling of violence between individuals. This is at best a negative sort of control, indicating that where people have enough room to avoid potential enemies, they have no need of the more elaborate ways of controlling violence. For example, von Fürer-Haimendorf recounts an 'administrative experiment' in which the Chenchus (hunter-gatherers) of Madras Presidency

were forcibly concentrated in large settlements administered by the Forest Department, and though their material conditions were greatly improved, they developed alarming social attitudes and rapidly lost their character as a peaceful and basically amiable people. Cases of murder, assault and rape multiplied, and the officials in charge of the settlements found themselves unable to control this tendency to violent crime. Yet there is an obvious explanation for this surprising development. Chenchu society, adjusted to lessen and remove friction by placing spatial distance between opponents, had no other machinery to restrain violence, and as men who had quarrelled or were rivals were prevented from getting out of each other's way, the traditional means of avoiding clashes could not operate.[1]

If, for purposes of social control, systems of dominance and territory in animals amount to sophisticated versions of avoidance, one would wish to know whether a similar equation could be drawn in human contexts. The same applies to gestures of appeasement in their rôle of 'cut-off' acts (see Chance's work, cited above, p. 86). We may recall Reynolds' suggestion (see p. 56) about the possible effects of hierarchical organization in allowing face-to-face contact to be evaded in overcrowded situations. But evidence on this point is at best conjectural, and in addition we are on dangerous theoretical ground. It would be naïve in the extreme to identify the idea of dominance, for example, with that of authority, although a study of interaction between the two might help to clarify the notion of charisma, and although in Chapter VIII I enquire what might be structurally common to both as organizing principles.

Leaving aside the links with social control through avoidance of prospective adversaries, one can consider hierarchy and territory as bare structural principles and speculate a little on their connections

[1] Von Fürer-Haimendorf 1967, p. 22.

with 'social control' in human societies. It evidently comes naturally to children to form relations of 'dominance' based partly on
fighting ability and partly on sheer self-confidence and bluff, and
these could well have the effect of reducing subsequent conflict. In
the case of children, the end-point of the social control exercised
by 'dominance' may be not the elimination of conflict but through
it the efficient organization of tasks or games. Wilson quotes a
Nyakyusa informant on the establishment of leaders among boys
who are later to form age-villages:

When we herd cows as boys . . . there is always one who is obeyed by
his fellows whatever he says. No one chooses him, he gains his leadership and his prestige by bodily strength. For always, when we are boys
together among the cows, we vie with one another and dispute about
going to turn back straying cattle, or about fetching fire to cook the food
we have brought with us. And so we start fighting, and we go on fighting
until one of us beats all his fellows completely and so becomes the leader
. . . And he is greatly respected. He settles quarrels too. What we
quarrel about most as boys is a particular insult: one says to another,
'You are only a child, you are, I am your senior.' This is always happening and then it is the part of the one who is leader to set those two on to
a fight. We all stand round and watch and the one who first cries is
proved the child.[1]

It has been argued that territorial organization is important in
reducing aggressive contact in human societies. It is certainly true
that the ownership of defended space brings with it the possibility
of withdrawing at will and hence of avoiding conflict—certainly of
controlling it; controlling it, that is, in the sense of regulating its
location and, up to a point, its incidence.

We come now to the rôle of ritualized acts and gestures in
fighting. I have hinted above that there is some uncertainty among
ethologists over the existence in man of a 'killing inhibition'
evoked by submissive behaviour on the part of a defeated adversary.
Indeed it is hard to see how this could be identified as a purely
'instinctive' response in man. It seems probable that the move of
appealing for mercy, while emphatically withdrawing from competition with the opponent, is a constant element of cultures, but
one needs a great deal more comparative evidence on this point.
Paradoxically, many social anthropologists take for granted that
there is in man, usually, a fundamental reluctance to kill, however

[1] Wilson 1951, p. 22.

it is acquired. They often explain acts of violence, for example, by pointing to events which have made people lose their 'normal' control. It looks as if any built-in inhibition there may be against killing can itself be temporarily suppressed, for instance by alcohol or fatigue. Anthropologists have given this as an explanation of crimes of violence. Elwin records the following case history:

Marvi Mundra and his wife came home very late one evening in October after working all day in the fields. When they reached the house, the girl at once began to cook their supper, and after a short time Mundra asked if it was ready. She said rather crossly that it was on the fire, and that directly it was ready she would give it to him. Mundra, exhausted by his long day in the fields and by the prospect of a still longer night watching the crops, lost his normal 'automatic control', picked up a stick from the fire and gave his wife three heavy blows which killed her.[1]

Southall assumes even more explicitly that some form of inhibition normally suppresses violence. In a sense this is obviously true, yet a more precise understanding of the kind of inhibition involved would do much to transform the following from a straightforward description into a hypothesis which could be tested:

In general, the factor of beer drinking, and in one case of *waragi* (illicit spirit) drinking, seems to represent a lowering of inhibitions, which permits violence to result from pre-existing differences not otherwise sufficient to cause it. The cases show men falling out with one another, when drunk, over idle boasting, mutual insults, and abuse about women, or trivial disputes over property, in one case while gambling.[2]

It is commonly assumed to be at this point that modern weapon technology makes nonsense of the biological controls on aggression in man: 'The analogue in man may be represented by submissive postures or crying which may evoke pity or inhibit an aggressor. In the modern scene, however, a bullet or a nuclear missile can kill a conspecific before he has any opportunity to appeal to any possibly inborn inhibitions in the aggressor.'[3] I have suggested that what weapons do is increasingly to eliminate the aggressive element from fighting and from warfare as well. There is also the possibility that the distance factor in modern weapons, by interfering selectively with the display and intimidation characteristic of face-to-face combat, affects the communicative aspect of fighting, but this could not be expected to happen in any simple

[1] Elwin 1943, p. 145.   [2] Southall 1960.   [3] Rifkin 1963.

manner. One story which I have come across depicts the very careful control of the procedure of a battle in such a way as to preserve the most personal, immediate and purposive elements of fighting—and hence perhaps to preserve its communicative elements as well as minimizing *unintentional* bloodshed:

According to tradition, the war between the two Euboean cities, Chalcis and Eretria, in the 7th century B.C. was fought wholly in the form of a contest. A solemn pact in which the rules were laid down was deposited beforehand in the temple of Artemis. The time and place for the encounter were then appointed. All missiles were forbidden; spears, arrows, slingstones; only the sword and the lance were allowed.[1]

If indeed we do possess—however we come by it—a powerful 'block' against destroying a helpless enemy, then perhaps one can draw some reason for optimism from the increasing quality of war journalism and particularly of war photography. The publicity of modern warfare is inevitably restoring the personal impact of violence, and thus seems likely to give the killing inhibition a chance to 'work'—among precisely the people who are in a position to take effective political action. So, paradoxically, the voters and demonstrators may be experiencing something more like 'biological' aggressiveness than are the generals. This point has been unaccountably ignored by ethologists writing about human conflict, who—despite Lorenz's 'Avowal of Optimism'—tend to be uniformly gloomy.

In connection with weapons, it is interesting to note the work of Kortlandt and Kooij on the use of objects by primates, both in captivity and in the wild. Both throwing and clubbing have been observed in chimpanzees. There is evidently some doubt about the dividing line between 'agonistic' throwing and clubbing, and intimidation displays, although in the case of throwing the authors treat the problem as one of accuracy of aim. Their general conclusion is:

(throwing and clubbing) . . . are obviously some kind of extensions or derivations of the general intimidation display that normally results from a conflict between aggression and fear. We may assume therefore that the rudimentary use of weapons shown by the great apes represents a secondary specialization which, in the course of evolution, has branched off from the rowdyism that is typical of the primate way of showing off.

[1] Huizinga 1949, p. 96.

Translated into human terms, this conclusion means that war-dancing is phylogenetically older than the shooting war, and that this in its turn is older than armed hunting.[1]

Thus, paradoxically, the use of weapons may be a phylogenetic consequence of aggressive display in an upright, large-brained primate living in the open. This adds significance to the suggestion made above that weapons alter the nature of display. But the paradox arises only if one assumes that the sole function of threatening displays is to replace actual fighting.

Gunboat diplomacy, on whatever scale, may often be effective in achieving one's object without having to fight, but there is no reason to suppose that ceremonious parades of strength are uniformly designed to replace combat; they seem just as likely to enhance pugnacity and provoke a fight. So it would often be more correct to regard war-dancing or the equivalent as an integral part of fighting, rather than as a substitute for it. This may be equally true of animal fights, as Barnett and Evans have argued:

The question is, to what extent do the postures and sounds, described as threatening, actually perfom these functions? . . . a phase of posturing followed by actual attack, may suggest that 'threatening' is a means of increasing the performer's readiness to attack: in other words that there is, initially at least, a positive feedback rather than a negative . . .[2]

I have emphasized that it is seldom possible to mark off 'ritualized' from 'real' combat in animals, and clearly this seems likely to be true of the human case. Whatever 'ritualization' amounts to, I do not believe it is typically an all-or-nothing affair, although ethologists frequently compare a ritualized gesture with its 'unritualized prototype', and although the degree of ritualization in an encounter can certainly change dramatically. Compare the following accounts:

In the triumph ceremony of geese, there is certainly quite a lot of autochthonous aggression, as can be demonstrated in the quasi-pathological case of homosexual gander pairs. In these, bond behaviour is much more intense than it ever is in normal heterosexual pairs, occasionally reaching a truly ecstatic climax . . . abnormally high intensity of ritualized activity causes true aggression in Freud's sense, that is to say a recrudescence of the phylogenetically older, unritualized behaviour patterns . . . ritualized redirection suddenly breaks down and the partners

[1] Kortlandt and Kooij 1963.   [2] Barnett & Evans 1965.

proceed to fight with a fury never otherwise observed in goose combat
... In homicide as every policeman knows, the loving spouse is the most
likely suspect, the word 'loving' emphatically not being used ironically.[1]

The Joluo people have a custom at marriages of 'pulling the girl' to the
village of the groom. Traditionally, the brothers and friends of the girl
should resist this 'capture'. In fact, however, the marriage has been
arranged by them and both parties are fully aware that this is a mock
battle. On occasion these fights become a spirited and serious 'free for
all'. From time to time, therefore, one or more of the party is seriously
injured and not infrequently death results . . . The authorities . . .
naturally prosecute in cases of this kind. The result is usually manslaughter, and the sentence is a light one.[2]

But these, I think, are best regarded as isolated cases on the
extremes of the ritualization dimension. It is doubtful whether
there is any such thing as totally unritualized fighting. We are in
a difficulty, of course, over the lack of a precise meaning for the
term 'ritualization'. But one thing the members of the Huxley
symposium did seem to agree on was the communicative aspect of
all 'ritualized' actions. One might indeed wish to define fighting in
terms of the communication brought about through reciprocal
display, thus contrasting true fighting with (for example) ambush-
ing an enemy and pouncing on him unawares.

The strong probability is that in both human and animal systems
agonistic display and attack are generally inseparable and represent
points of emphasis in the same process, rather than alternatives.
This is yet another indication that fighting is a far from hap-
hazard business. The really uncontrolled aggressive brawl is
probably equally rare in animal and human society, resulting when
it occurs from a breakdown of structure and hence of control at
some level of micro- or macro-organization. Uncontrolled human
warfare is, as I have suggested, a different matter.

SOCIAL CONTROL

Towards the beginning of this chapter, I gave some examples of
anthropological definitions of 'social control', and discussed in
more detail the view of social control implicit in Malinowski's
Crime and Custom in Savage Society. It is in the tradition of British

[1] Lorenz 1964.
[2] Wilson 1960. Bohannan adds (ibid., p. 231) that when this happens, the
Joluo make 'ritual and domestic adjustments, not predominantly jural ones'.

and French sociology to treat social institutions and the human tendencies they are designed to control, as belonging to entirely separate areas of discourse. I wish to suggest now that this assumption ought to be reconsidered, because it does not allow for the elaborate and interconnected ways in which behaviour, by its nature, is controlled and organized at every point.

For the purpose of ethological comparison, I restricted the field to the 'social control' of aggression, and considered what an ethologist might make of this idea. This made it necessary to summarize a good deal of literature, much of it controversial, on the nature of aggression in animals and the various factors which are said to keep bloodshed to a minimum in intra-specific conflict. The conclusion was that the term 'social control' in relation to aggression in animals should make sense to an ethologist, for a number of reasons. On a molar level, the aggressive impulse in species which possess it forms an indispensable link in the basic social structure, and is frequently 'controlled' through the logic of this structure. On a molecular level, the aggressive impulse is itself balanced and controlled by the rest of the motivational structure which contributes to the animal's repertoire of social behaviour.[1] Furthermore, the procedure of fighting is organized and given regularity and structure by 'ritualized' elements which pervade it throughout, although they may be given greater or lesser emphasis at different points in the sequence of a fight. This last point may be made in functional terms, and usually is, by saying that natural selection has found a way of preserving the advantages of aggression while minimizing destructive violence by allowing fighting to be 'ritualized' into display. This is probably all right, except that it understates the displaying and communicating aspects of fighting itself. But for a more general account of 'social control' in animals we have to link the idea of control with that of structure. In the long run, aggression and fighting are controlled because they are structured and contribute to structure. This goes beyond the

---

[1] Cf. Chance (in preparation): '. . . the drives subserving sociability form a complex. Aggression does not, except at high intensities, disperse animals of the same species, but rather brings them together; in a variety of ways it is held in balance with flight tendencies and this balance is manifested in ambivalent postures, such as the upright and sideways postures of the rat. The mating drive also brings animals together, and so probably does a tendency towards social investigation which has not yet been fully analysed . . . above all, sociability depends on a sufficient availability of social submission.'

limited issue of aggression. The topic of aggression was chosen largely because the presence of aggression as an 'instinctive' impulse looked as if it presented a problem in the organization of a society whose solution needed some special explanation, but this is probably not so. Ultimately the clue to 'social control' in animals is to be found in the analysis of 'social structure'.

Now something very like this seems to be true of 'social control' in human societies, both in relation to aggression and more broadly. Keeping to aggression for the moment, we can see, for example from Evans-Pritchard's account of fighting among the Nuer how, despite the marked bellicosity of these people, the consequences of fighting are usually kept under control through the imposition of structure and organization at every point:

As Nuer are very prone to fighting, people are frequently killed. Indeed it is rare that one sees a senior man who does not show marks of club or spear . . . A Nuer will at once fight if he considers that he has been insulted, and they are very sensitive and easily take offence. When a man feels that he has suffered an injury there is no authority to whom he can make a complaint and from whom he can obtain redress, so he at once challenges the man who has wronged him to a duel and the challenge must be accepted. There is no other way of settling a dispute and a man's courage is his only immediate protection against aggression. Only when kinship or age-set status inhibits an appeal to arms does a Nuer hesitate to utter a challenge, for it does not occur to him to ask advice first, and no-one would listen to unsolicited advice.

. . . Boys fight with spiked bracelets. Men of the same village or camp fight with clubs, for it is a convention that spears must not be used between close neighbours lest one of them be killed and the community be split by a blood-feud. It is also a convention that no third person may take part in the fight, even though he be a close kinsman of one of the combatants. Once a fight has begun neither party can give way and they have to continue until one or the other is badly injured unless, as generally happens, people pull them away from each other, loudly protesting, and then stand between them.

When a fight starts between persons of different villages it is with the spear; every adult male of both communities takes part in it, and it cannot be stopped before considerable loss of life has ensued. Nuer know this and, unless they are very angry, are reluctant to start a fight with a neighbouring village and are often willing to allow a leopard-skin chief or the elders to intervene.[1]

[1] Evans-Pritchard 1940, pp. 151-2.

As far as 'social control' in general is concerned, the idea that the nature of social control is rooted in the fact of social organization is probably implied in Park and Burgess's definition of 'social control', which I quoted among others earlier on (p. 75). Such an idea would not be new in social anthropology. What we may learn from the ethological comparison is that conceptualized, institutional controls on behaviour represent the most conspicuous parts of a complex continuum of processes—and these processes are 'controlled' because they are structured, at every point at which one cares to analyse them. 'Social control' cannot be defined (except arbitrarily) in exclusively anthropological terms, because the definition must take into account the fact that institutional controls on behaviour merge and interact with the controlled and structured nature of this same behaviour. How this happens exactly is a matter for further research. Anthropology has traditionally accepted that social facts are interrelated in complicated ways. Where it has been mistaken, I suggest, is in failing to recognize that these complex interrelations do not stop short at an undifferentiated—and bogus—'human nature', but form a continuum with the equally complex elements of social organization and control which we partly share with other social species.

VII

ON GREETING

IN Chapter VI (p. 80) I touched on the question of ritual and ceremonial in human society, and its relation to processes of 'ritualization' both in animal social life and in human behaviour at the level of individual response. There are good reasons for not tackling such a topic head-on in a work of this kind—among them being the need for competence in a variety of relevant disciplines, and the lack of a vocabulary which does not threaten to prejudge the very relationship one sets out to investigate. Of course, this task will sooner or later have to be done, if there is felt to be any future in pursuing contacts between animal and human sociology. In the meantime, it seems worthwhile to consider, not 'ritual' as an unwieldy whole, but some of the 'minor' rules and ceremonies of everyday life, their continuities and divergences from one society to another, and the possibility that ethological studies may aid the social scientist in (a) noticing and (b) understanding them. Mary Douglas has written: 'For us, ... everyday symbolic enactment ... provides a focussing mechanism, a method of mnemonics and a control for experience.'[1] Yet these everyday observances are likely to escape the attention of the anthropological fieldworker unless they are conspicuous by their strangeness, in which case they will be treated as belonging to a 'foreign' symbolic system. Certainly there is room for much cultural diversity in the structuring of social interactions at this everyday level.[2] Yet it is possible that differences between societies in day-to-day social enactment have been exaggerated and wrongly interpreted. We are relatively un-observant about our own everyday rituals and about those of other societies when they resemble our own, and this may have led us to obscure the essential unity of systems which may constitute 'universals' of human society. What-

[1] Douglas 1966, pp. 62–3.
[2] See e.g. Hall's article on differences in 'individual distance' between different communities; and in their systems governing social life, such as the length of the socially relevant unit of time. Hall 1955.

ever the truth of this, it is undeniable that this area of social life—
the relatively unimpressive kind, together with the rules which
govern it—has been neglected in comparison with areas more
formalized and, perhaps, more accessible to conscious description
and prescription. As Goffman says,

. . . the study of ordinary human traffic and the patterning of ordinary
social contacts, has been little considered. It is well recognized, for
instance, that mobs can suddenly emerge from the peaceful flow of
human traffic, if conditions are right. But little consideration seems to
have been given to the question of what structure this peaceful intercourse possesses when mob formation is not an issue.[1]

Because the systems of behaviour under discussion are apt to be
overlooked most of the time, one suffers from a lack of documen-
tary material on the anthropological side. But such behaviour is
also comparatively unselfconscious, and this brings certain com-
pensating advantages. Hall,[2] writing of 'proxemic' systems, claims
that these differ from the more conventional subject-matter of
anthropology in that, once learned, they 'are maintained largely
out of conscious awareness' and hence cannot be elicited by simple
questioning. One may challenge the assumption that the systems
and models of social life which anthropologists traditionally
construct have to be accessible to the consciousness of the people
concerned. But Hall's point is that it is particularly useful to study
behaviour of this 'unselfconscious' type because of the relative
absence of distortions due, perhaps, to attempts at conscious
interpretation. If the everyday ceremonial behaviour we are about
to discuss is both systematic and relatively unselfconscious, it
provides a particularly attractive field in which to experiment with
ethological comparisons. In describing such action we can approximate to an ethological picture, more closely than in other areas
of human social activity whose conscious representations and
manipulations must continually be taken into account. And yet,
let it be noted, we are not thereby committed to any theory of the
unconscious mind. We are still firmly within the field of anthropology, if this is guaranteed by our being undeniably concerned with
a class of 'social facts'—the ceremonial structuring of interactions.
Out of this rather vaguely defined corpus of small-scale everyday social ceremony, I propose to select the more restricted

---

[1] Goffman 1963, p. 4.   [2] Hall 1963.

category of 'greeting ceremonies' and their significance in ordering animal and human interactions. It may, however, be thought that 'greeting' begs a number of questions by being an 'achievement word'[1] instead of denoting the bare characteristics of the situations in which the behaviour occurs. We do not know what if anything is achieved by 'greeting'. So I shall also refer, if clumsily, to 'meeting' behaviour and ceremonies, it being understood that extensionally speaking I mean by this term the class of behaviour which both ethologists and observers of human conduct tend to call 'greeting'.

MEETING CEREMONIES AND THEIR PHYLOGENY

Ceremonies and gestures of 'greeting' have been described as such for a number of subhuman species, chiefly among the birds,[2] carnivores[3] and primates.[4] Unfortunately 'greeting' as an analytical category of behaviour has not, apparently, been systematically worked out. This may be an instance of ethologists adopting a concept a little uncritically, misled by its seemingly self-evident place in human social relations. That is, 'greeting' may belong among terms like 'leadership' or even 'dominance' itself, whose use in ethology has recently been criticized by Chance.[5] There seems little that is common to 'lipsmacking' and 'presenting' in primates and the 'triumph ceremony' in geese, except the 'greeting' function which each is said to have, and we are not told what this function is. Clearly the non-ethologist is on shaky ground here. But the fact that the term 'greeting' occurs so frequently in the literature of animal behaviour, without any apparent consensus on its status as a causal, functional or descriptive concept, surely indicates a lurking assumption that (crudely put) 'everybody knows' what is meant by greeting. Many occurrences of the term 'greeting' in ethology may be products of the 'aha!-reaction' I criticized in Chapter IV. Yet if 'greeting' is an achievement word—and it

---

[1] I do not claim that 'greeting' fits exactly into Ryle's class of 'achievement words' (*The Concept of Mind*, 1949, pp. 149–53) but it looks more like a 'got-it word' in Ryle's sense than an objective label for a class of actions regularly observed in specified situations.

[2] See e.g. Hinde 1961, and Ch. 11 of Lorenz 1966.

[3] See e.g. Etkin 1964 and Hediger 1955.

[4] See e.g. Andrew 1963, Hall 1962, van Hooff 1967, Wickler 1967.

[5] Chance 1967.

may be a perfectly legitimate one—what exactly is accomplished in greeting has not, to my knowledge, been spelled out. Consider for example Andrew's description of 'friendly', 'defensive', 'close', and 'distant' greeting in primates and their analogues in passerine birds;[1] or Etkin's remark that in wolves, 'friendly greetings with tail wagging and howling are frequently exchanged between members of the pack, particularly on social occasions, as when the pack gathers together before going off on a hunt.'[2] It therefore seems likely that investigation of what is common to both human and animal 'greeting' may help to show whether 'greeting' really has a place even in ethological vocabulary—or whether a variety of different terms, such as 'appeasement' or 'contact gesture' would be less misleading. These are equally, but more overtly, 'got-it words', and for this reason they carry the possibility of distinguishing between what the gesture is 'designed' to achieve and what its effect may be in particular cases.

Proceeding, as we must, a little introspectively, we can suggest that what distinguishes greeting within the wider class of human everyday ceremonial interactions is its association with an encounter or 'meeting' however defined, and we can surmise that this is what impels ethologists to speak of 'greeting' in animals as well. The questions then arise whether there is such a unitary class of 'meeting ceremonies' in animal and human societies, extensionally equivalent to 'greeting', and in what does its unity consist; does it for example have a common phylogeny, and how is its actual place in the larger system of social behaviour, related to its phylogeny? We may add a proviso that species in which to look for meeting ceremonies must be those whose social structure allows or relies on recognition of individuals—i.e. in which 'the known individual' is in a significant category among conspecifics. The distinction common in human greeting between strangers and acquaintances has its equivalents in, for example, dogs[3] and Chacma baboons.[4] It is necessary for the moment to treat as if it were a

---

[1] Andrew 1963.   [2] Etkin 1964.
[3] See e.g. Scott & Fuller 1965, pp. 76–7. See also Chance's comment on an article of Reynolds' :'. . . it should now be incumbent on those able to make observations on this point to make every effort to establish whether [chimpanzees] do greet strangers differently from the members of groups with which they repeatedly associate, and if so, what constitutes the difference.' Chance 1967 *Man* N.S. 2,1,130.
[4] Hall 1962. This author describes how through a series of 'greetings' an experimentally introduced tame male was incorporated into the wild troop.

single category all the behaviour which ethologists label 'greeting'. The fact that ethologists do speak of 'greeting' in very different species, provides a temporary justification for making this assumption—which will at least enable us to assemble the evidence. We avoid the danger of question-begging, by trying to discover exactly what, if anything, is common to behaviours which are called 'greeting'. It will not be surprising if we find that different evolutionary causes are responsible for this behaviour in widely differing species—indeed this may support the belief that we are dealing with a significant category, given independent evidence for the existence of such a category. A remark of Lorenz's is often quoted, that 'it is convergences which call attention to functional problems.' One could add that they also call attention to structural analogies. I propose, then, to make a deliberately naïve assumption that what is called 'greeting' in various species is, in some sense, 'the same thing'; and then to ask what actual identities there are which would justify this assumption.

One finds in the literature reference to meeting ceremonies in different species, linked apparently with a number of different behavioural systems. Some examples may be given.

In species whose social life is largely governed by dominance hierarchies, one would expect meetings between individuals to be marked by performance of the dominance-submission ritual or some version of it; this frame of reference may well overshadow any additional 'greeting' significance the gesture may have. This seems to be the case with dogs (and possibly with wolves in the wild). Thus one can guess from the observations of Scott and Fuller that encounters between strange dogs differ according to the dominance rôle which each is disposed to adopt. This in turn can depend on a number of factors, such as the site of the encounter:

If two strange animals approach each other on neutral territory, each walks slowly and stiff-leggedly towards the other, tail held straight up and waving slightly from side to side. They touch noses and then may cautiously nose each other's tail and genital region. Such behaviour may lead to mutual acceptance but more often results in an attack by one animal or the other.

. . . Another pattern [of dominance behaviour] is exhibited by a strange animal, approaching in a subordinate way. The stranger turns his head away, his eyes closed and ears held back, and attempts to make close contact with the other animal by weaving around him and leaping in the air with the back curved. This behaviour is often described as 'courting' and indicates a friendly approach.[1]

Yet several writers speak quite freely of 'greeting' in canines, and the question once more arises whether this is an informal, somewhat anthropomorphic use of words, or whether 'greeting' in these animals really does mean something more than the dominance-submission behaviour from which it is undoubtedly derived. Consider for example the passage from Etkin's paper, quoted above. Again Hediger, writing of interspecific social relations, says

In domestic animals the sometimes tiresome 'snout pushing' of a dog is well-known but at the same time is still often misunderstood. When two acquainted dogs meet each other the socially inferior animal has to touch the dominant one on the snout. Now, especially when meeting its master again after a long separation, the dog simply must jump at him to fulfil the greetings ceremony because its master's nose is so high above the ground.[2]

The 'triumph ceremony' of geese (notably the greylag goose, *Anser anser*) is something of a special case. Its significance goes far deeper than what we commonly understand by 'greeting'; it evidently constitutes a basic source of social organization in the species. It seems, however, from Lorenz's account that one way of looking at the 'triumph ceremony' is as a gesture of 'greeting' between members of a closely united family group. We may accept the authority of his claim (based on comparative and ontogenetic evidence) that the 'cackling' component of this ceremony has evolved through the ritualization of a redirected threatening display.[3]

The primates show a rich variety of behaviour occurring in 'meeting' situations and labelled 'greeting'. Goodall's account will illustrate the kind of subtle distinctions which chimpanzees seem able to make in 'greeting'. If 'greeting' is legitimately taken to be a single category of action, then in these animals it clearly provides an idiom whereby a large number of different relationships can be expressed.

When two temporary associations come together certain forms of behaviour are observed that are not normally apparent in intra-group interactions, and this behaviour varies with the age and sex composition

---

[1] Scott & Fuller 1965, pp. 76–7.   [2] Hediger 1965.
[3] see Lorenz 1966, Ch. 11, esp pp. 156-9.

of each group. If there is a mature male in each, there is normally a certain amount of excitement, which is greater when more males are present. Males may drum on tree trunks with their hands or feet, shake branches, run along slapping the ground with their hands, or call loudly . . . These displays may continue for as long as five minutes. Similar behaviour is seen when a lone male joins the group.

When crossing open country towards a group some distance away but within earshot, males frequently break into a run, slapping the ground, moving bipedally, hitting out at branches, and calling loudly.

On approaching a food tree in which another group containing one or more males is feeding, each member of the arriving group usually pauses for about half a minute on a low branch and then climbs up and approaches and greets one or more of the chimps in the tree, its place on the low branch being taken by the next newcomer. If the group established in the tree consists of females and juveniles only, members of another group do not pause before climbing up.

. . . There are several ways in which one chimp may 'greet' another, depending on the length of time they have been separated, the degree of mutual attraction, and their mood at the time.

The most common greeting [occurs when] one chimpanzee goes up to another and reaches out to touch it with the flat of the hand or with the back of the slightly flexed fingers. The top of the head, shoulder, back, groin, thigh or genital area may be touched in greeting. A female in oestrus is normally touched on her sexual swelling in greeting; a male may also put his face to her genital area as though sniffing.

Greater mutual attraction is shown when two animals move towards each other with soft panting grunts and touch each other. Another form of greeting occurs when a male stands upright, one arm above his head, while another runs towards him. The two then fling their arms about each other. In both forms of greeting (above) a male normally has an erection of the penis.[1]

Other recent work has concentrated on establishing the phylo-genetic sources of primate displays, including 'greeting' displays. Van Hooff, for example, describes in detail the 'lip-smacking face' in many catarrhine monkeys, which is clearly associated with the 'functional' lipsmacking found in grooming situations:

In most species, the movement is not frequently seen between animals which are associated in an established relationship with one another . . . It may be shown, however, quite frequently during a short time when the animals meet for the first time, or after a period of separation . . . An approach is followed by mutual grooming, huddling together, play,

[1] Goodall 1965.

mating or simply being in each other's neighbourhood . . . As a rule the posture facilitates non-hostile approach between the individuals and this may be achieved by an appeasing or reassuring effect on the partner . . .[1]

Van Hooff himself does not use the term 'greeting', but analyses the display in terms of a combination of 'appeasing', 'reassuring' and 'attracting' functions.

Sexual displays provide another origin of 'greeting' behaviour in primates, as Darwin noted in his own distinctive way: 'The habit of turning the hinder end as a greeting to an old friend or new acquaintance, which seems to us so odd, is not really more so than the habits of many savages, for instance that of rubbing their bellies with their hand, or rubbing noses together.'[2] Wickler discusses the rôle of presentation as a 'greeting ceremony' and its development from a specific invitation to mate, to a generalized 'submissive' display. He seems partly to equate 'greeting' with 'appeasement' or the reduction of aggression on the part of group members, by the provocation of a (possibly sub-threshold) sexual response. This, in his view, partly explains the presence in some male primates of structures which appear to 'imitate' the female sexual swellings.

The meeting rituals so far discussed derive, then, from several phylogenetic sources; the ritualized redirection of aggression away from the partner (geese—and some fish—see *On Aggression*, pp. 145–7); 'infantile' submission (canines); grooming (primates) and 'sexual' submission (primates, and also felines—see Wickler's paper). These can be brought under the one head of 'appeasement' if what this means is that the 'greeting' gesture allows 'meeting' to take place by avoiding or suppressing the aggressive (sometimes the fleeing) response which an approach might otherwise be expected to provoke. Another possible evolutionary source of 'greeting' rituals must be considered, because of its putative relation to human greeting: the imprinting/following complex of behaviour. Gray, for example, suggests that '. . . the smiling response in human infants is the motor equivalent of the following response in animals below the higher primates.'[3] Ainsworth

---

[1] Van Hooff 1967.
[2] Darwin, Charles 1876. Sexual selection in relation to monkeys. Nature 15; 18–19. Cited by Wickler 1967.
[3] Gray 1958.

observed arm-raising and handclapping 'in greeting' in Ganda babies of 21 and 32 weeks respectively; and writes: 'After the child is able to crawl he is likely to terminate his greeting by crawling to the loved person as quickly as he is able.'[1] Hinde, discussing the importance of social (smiling, cuddling etc) as opposed to material rewards in setting up the bond between mother and child, concludes: "The apparent importance of these social patterns is reminiscent of the greeting ceremonies of geese and other species, and of the way in which young nidifugous birds will learn to follow a particular model without receiving any of the conventional rewards.'[2] Lorenz, on the other hand, believes that the human greeting smile is a direct analogue of the triumph ceremony, that it is 'originally' a gesture of appeasement through the ritualized redirection of a threat.[3] Tinbergen adopts this explanation of the present rôle of human greeting, although he is less sure about its phylogeny: 'It is interesting to see how human beings, on the level of reason, have evolved similar ceremonies. 'Greeting', whatever its psychological basis may be, often has the function of appeasement, of suppressing aggressiveness and related reactions, and thus opening the gate for further contact.'[4] In considering human greeting, of course, we need to know what components or functions are common to the various greeting procedures in different societies; the greeting smile, taken implicitly by several ethologists as a 'basic' and universal form of greeting, may or may not be so.[5]

There is ample support for the view that a ritualized act can supersede its phylogeny in the sense of acquiring properties of an independent drive with its own appetitive and releasing mechanisms. I touched on this topic of 'emancipation' in Chapter VI. This has been asserted particularly strongly in the case of birds.[6] When this happens the phylogenetic history of the rite becomes

---

[1] Ainsworth 1963.   [2] Hinde 1961.   [3] Lorenz 1966, p. 152.
[4] Tinbergen 1953, p. 48.
[5] A link was once claimed to exist between submissive presenting in primates, and prostitution in human society—see Sahlins (1959) who rejects the idea. It might be fun, if equally fanciful, to speculate on analogies between asexual presentation (discussed above) and the greeting kiss in ourselves. Henriques, describing how the 'kiss of salutation' has varied in popularity over time and space, quotes Congreve's *The Way of the World*: 'You think you're in the country where great lubberly brothers slabber and kiss one another when they meet, like a call of Serjeant's—'Tis not the fashion here . . .' Henriques, Fernando 1959: *Love in Action* (Panther edn) 1964, p. 124.
[6] See e.g. Lorenz 1966 & 1964.

partly irrelevant to the explanation of its present rôle in the social organization. The case is less clear at the level of the non-human primates, which have not until recently been popular subjects for 'classical' ethological research. But one would intuitively expect that in these animals, whose mental and social organization allows far more sophisticated individual relations than are found in most other groups, the gestures expressing and defining these relations would be correspondingly divorced from the simpler motivational conflicts from which they appear to derive. Thus Hediger describes 'asexual erection' as part of the 'greeting ceremony' of cebus monkeys, and asserts that 'the sexual function has gone and been replaced by a purely social one.'[1] Wickler also distinguishes clearly between the 'sexual' and 'social' versions of the signals he describes (though admittedly he equates 'greeting' with 'appeasement').[2]

The case would be more convincing if we could include *Homo sapiens* among the primates for the purpose of showing that 'greeting' is functionally independent of its origins. But this would be to prejudge the comparability of human greeting with what is called 'greeting' in other species. So we must simply say that there is a fairly good case to be made for the following suppositions; (a) that meeting rituals in several animal groups, in spite of disparate evolutionary sources, could be drawn together in some account which might justify the common label 'greeting'; (b) that even if the apparently diverse phylogenetic origins of 'greeting' can be assimilated to some such functional category as 'appeasement', this does not exhaust all discussion of 'greeting'. By this I mean that even if all 'greeting' springs (phylogenetically speaking) from different ways of fulfilling a common need in social animals to 'appease' a possibly hostile conspecific, the concept of 'emancipation' entitles us to look for quite new and original ways in which 'greeting' procedures may be utilized in social organization. I am not sure whether it is ultimately valid to discuss meeting rituals in animals outside the framework of motivational conflict, but in any case an attempt to do so may help to make clear what is significant about human greeting. One would not claim that greeting ceremonies in human societies function uniquely in dispelling actual hostile impulses in the individuals greeted, nor indeed that their social and institutional significance can be exhaustively stated on a

[1] Hediger 1965.   [2] Wickler 1967.

psychological model of the approach/avoidance type. So if we are to find any interesting formulations to span human and animal 'greeting', it seems worth adopting a 'micro-sociological' frame of reference; i.e. we are looking at small-scale (if very repetitive) events and interactions, but relating them firmly to supra-individual structures rather than internal motivational systems.

MEETING CEREMONIES AS 'SIGNALS'

It appears to be characteristic of at least Western European society, that meetings and partings between individuals and small groups are noticeably 'structured' (in the sense of being predictable and 'ritualized') in relation to other everyday social behaviour. This goes beyond the obvious and variable rules about handshaking and so forth, and involves a whole network of prescribed behaviour ranging from the most formal and institutionalized to the most minute and momentary—but apparently essential—actions. As far as meetings are concerned, Goffman's vocabulary of 'situational presence' is an excellent way of characterizing the 'meeting situation.'[1] This vocabulary might in fact usefully be tried out in certain ethological contexts. The general concept of 'situational proprieties' for example, as well as of 'interaction tonus' and the idea of being interactionally 'in play', promises to make excellent sense in dealing with primates and (possibly) wolves;[2] and something very like 'civil inattention' seems to be important in the social organization of domestic cats[3]. Certainly a clear idea of the kind of 'presence' established by 'greeting' in different animal species would provide much firmer ground for comparisons of human and animal greeting. Moreover, a full understanding of this 'situational presence' would go a long way towards clearing up the concept of 'effective social contact' which was a source of puzzlement in Chapter v.

One feels considerably safer in the human than the animal case, in trying to work out what is special about greeting. Even so, much of the argument must be speculative—even introspective in the

[1] Goffman 1963. Indeed one way of describing greeting in our society may be as a means of easing the transition between 'unfocused' and 'focused' interaction in Goffman's sense.

[2] See e.g. Hediger's citing of Schenkel's paper (1965).

[3] See e.g. Leyhausen 1965.

sense of drawing on common experience of a particular culture—
because for the reasons given at the beginning of this chapter,
comparative ethnographic evidence is hard to come by. If, on an
analysis such as Goffman's, we can tighten up the concept of the
'meeting situation' by describing it as an operation in the course
of which the participants in an encounter become 'present' to one
another in a special way, then it may also be possible to distinguish
'greeting' from other behaviour incidental to it, in terms of setting
up this situation. Goffman himself (thinking primarily of cases
where the meeting ritual comprises the whole of the encounter)
suggests such a distinction:

In our own middle-class society there are 'chats' where two individuals
pause in their separate lines of action for what both recognize to be a
necessarily brief period of time; there are greetings, whereby communion
is established and maintained long enough for the participants to exchange brief interpersonal rituals; and briefest of all, there are recognitional or 'friendly' glances . . . except for the ritual of civil inattention,
the mere exchange of friendly glances is perhaps the most frequent of
our interpersonal rituals.[1]

Goffman thus restricts the term 'greeting' to verbal exchanges
which establish the 'situational presence' necessary for more prolonged interaction. But it does seem that verbal greeting, however
formal and lengthy, has something in common with the briefest of
recognitional nods which the 'chat' does not essentially share.[2]
One pointer to this is the 'clearance function' which Goffman
ascribes to these minimal signs but which applies as well to verbal
greeting. But a more general reason why verbal greeting and

[1] Goffman 1963, p. 101.
[2] One difference between verbal greeting and recognitional gestures is, however, evident from Goffman's argument. As he says (pp. 13–14), in Western
society one cannot typically be held responsible or challenged on a non-verbal
display. Indeed it is often difficult to make a challenge stick, even where the
display is far from minimal and has a well-understood 'meaning'. (Cf. *Romeo and
Juliet*, Act 1, sc. 1:
—I will frown as I pass by, and let them take it as they list.
. . .—Do you bite your thumb at us, sir?
—I do bite my thumb, sir.
—Do you bite your thumb at us, sir?
—etc., and the brawl can only begin when someone lets himself be drawn into a
'quotable' insult). This allows much variety in the giving and acknowledging of
minimal gestures, to express for example subtle degress of super- and sub-
ordination—which is not true of verbal greeting. If someone makes a verbal
overture he commits himself publicly; and to ignore him or keep him waiting
is a publicly hostile act.

recognitional gestures seem to belong together, has something to
do with their informational content and the kind of message they
convey. If we treat greeting conversations as belonging to a simple
and straightforward model of communication, then they are almost
completely redundant. This fact was noted in a colloquial way by
Trotter:

> Conversations of greeting are naturally particularly rich in the exchange
> of purely ceremonial remarks, ostensibly based on some subject like the
> weather, in which there must necessarily be an absolute community of
> knowledge. It is possible, however, for a long conversation to be made
> up entirely of similar elements, and to contain no trace of any conveyance
> of new ideas; such intercourse is probably that which on the whole is
> most satisfying to the 'normal' man and leaves him more comfortably
> stimulated than would originality or brilliance, or any other manifesta-
> tion of the strange and therefore of the disreputable.[1]

One is tempted to argue that verbal greeting, despite its surface
similarity to other forms of utterance, differs qualitatively from any
kind of message—perhaps does not belong in a communication
model of language at all. Berne, with emphasis on the psychological
implications, has put forward a model for these 'non-informative'
exchanges ('if you are not stroked, your spinal cord will shrivel
up') which rings true in an amusing way.[2] Greeting on this view,
whether verbal or not, would amount to an exchange of 'strokes';
different gestures or utterances would have different 'stroke' values,
and the number of 'strokes' required would depend both on individual needs and on external features of the situation. This line of
argument is attractive, too, to anyone trying to link human and
animal 'greeting', since it seems to excuse one from considering the
unique features of human language. But it would be quite wrong to
try to separate actual utterances into the informative and the totally
non-informative, of which the latter include verbal greeting and
only the former are to have the status of messages.[3] Berne's

---

[1] Trotter 1916, p. 119.

[2] Berne 1966, especially Chapter 3. Cf. also Morris (1967, pp. 204f.) on
'Grooming talk'.

[3] There is, however, an important insight to be drawn from Berne's treatment
of greeting. Human greeting, in the psychological sphere, is related to motivational systems and social development. Equally, in the context of societies,
greeting has parallels with gift-giving and other forms of exchange. This last
is independent of the connection between ceremonial greetings and the institutions of which they are often a part, for both formal and informal greetings are
essentially systematic and reciprocal.

'pastimes' for example ('Kitchen', 'Wardrobe', 'General Motors', etc) belong in some intermediate category, and other examples can be found. The most stereotyped of informal greeting exchanges may contain some (not too much) information about the weather, or people's state of health. But more importantly, to try to characterize verbal greeting as non-informative in a communication-theory sense would be to go too far in the borrowing of terms belonging properly to a mathematical system; it is difficult to see how evidence in support of such a statement could be quantified. The most that can be suggested, I suspect, is that greeting utterances are predominantly non-informative in a rather old-fashioned sense, and that they are not primarily concerned with the straightforward transmission of semantic information. To this extent they belong not with other grammatical indicatives and interrogatives but with non-verbal greetings and recognitional gestures. Yet even this must not be taken too strictly. At another level of analysis, both human (verbal and non-verbal) and animal greetings contain—even if they do not convey—information of a kind. The following discussion is intended to show that the kind of information encapsulated in 'greeting' ceremonies may be rather similar in each case.

MEETING CEREMONIES AS MEDIATORS OF 'STRUCTURE'

The above argument points toward a negative definition of greeting as we experience it in human society. In the meeting situation, greeting ceremonies may be messages, but not of a straightforward kind; they may indeed belong to a different, more primitive code from those which underlie ordinary linguistic communication. What I wish to suggest is that a model could be developed to account for 'greeting' in animals, linking it (roughly) to the structuring of social time and space, and of the broader dimensions of social relationships themselves. Such a model, properly worked out, would provide the justification I was seeking above for speaking of 'greeting' in species taxonomically so far apart. If it turns out that similar principles distinguish human greeting, whether verbal or not, this would be yet another example of the use and re-use in human societies of systems whose structural elements are provided biologically.

Goodall's account, quoted above, of wild chimpanzees shows

plainly that the form and intensity of the 'greeting' ceremony can be influenced by the length of time the animals have been separated.[1] This seems to be the case with a number of primates,[2] with dogs (at least in their interspecific relations with man),[3] with horses[4] and with geese.[5] That it is also true of our own greeting is a matter of common experience. Goffman writes, for example: '. . . each engagement tends to be initiated with an amount of fuss appropriate to the period of lapsed contact, and terminated with the amount appropriate to the assumed period of separation. There results a kind of tiding over, and a compensation for the diminishing effects of separation.'[6] That we are dealing with social rather than any other kind of time, is indicated by the fact that the effect of separation time on the greeting procedure is not lineal. It tends to diminish progressively with increased time, perhaps reaching some kind of an asymptote. In the case of many animals a limit would be set by their moderate powers of memory and recognition, and the consequent breakdown of the social relationship altogether after a given period of separation. But within the temporal span of acquaintanceship, as it were, possible for each species, if social time is structured at this level in terms of encounters and the gaps between them then the 'greeting' ceremony provides an excellent focus for encapsulating this structure and marking out the points of change within it. Human society, of course, provides an indefinite number of ways of dividing up social time, and a man's use of the greeting ceremony may additionally indicate which scale he is operating in.

There are a number of ways of imposing a social structure on physical space; territorial divisions represent one such system. Carpenter writes: '. . . it would seem that the 'perceptual-cognitive

---

[1] Goodall's description should be interpreted with reference to Reynolds & Reynolds (1965). At the end of their paper these authors tentatively endorse a suggestion of Calhoun's that despite appearances chimpanzees do have a highly organized social structure. The various long-range vocalizations and displays, it seems, may be centrally important in maintaining and expressing this overall structure, which subsumes the small fluid groupings that are actually seen in the field.

[2] See Andrew 1963.

[3] See e.g. Hediger 1965.

[4] See e.g. Hafez et al. 1962.

[5] See e.g. Lorenz 1966, Ch. 11. Given the ethological view of the rite as acquiring its own consummatory component, this is also explicable on quite a simple drive-reduction theory of the Hullian type.

[6] Goffman 1963, p. 102.

maps' or behaviour systems of animals, if and when they are charted, will more accurately represent territorial behaviour than merely geographical or space maps.'[1]—and Klopfer and Hailman remark that with systems of territory and individual distance '. . . a periphery is created at which contact with other individuals may occur.'[2] Another example, this time of the social structuring of microspace in human encounters, is the set of 'proxemic' systems analysed by Hall.[3] It seems well established that many animals use gestures and vocalizations to organize and express spatial relationships within a group; see e.g. Andrew's discussion of 'close' and 'distant' contact calls in passerine birds and primates.[4] Andrew associates primate greeting with the former. 'Close' and 'distant contact' appears to indicate a socially relevant division of space in several species; the latter marked by low-intensity behaviour of the 'I am here' type[5] and the former by more intensive mutual attention and interaction and characterized by the performance of 'greeting' ceremonies. The dimensions of individual distance, in species where it operates, are clearly important in this connection.[6] But it would be difficult to decide how relevant the ethological notion of individual distance is to human social life, beyond noting that there are minimum distances at which people feel comfortable together, and that these are subject to cultural variation.[7] It is evident, too, that the establishment of 'mutual presence' in Goffman's sense makes a huge difference to the human (at least

---

[1] Carpenter 1958. [2] Klopfer & Hailman 1967, p. 141.

[3] Hall 1963. Hall's discussion of the '-emic' and '-etic' factors in these uses of space clearly has a bearing on whether the 'greeting' and other systems under discussion are to be treated as 'codes' in a strict sense—a question which I prefer to leave open.

[4] Andrew 1963.

[5] See e.g. Lorenz 1966, p. 176; and Schaller 1965.

[6] The concept of individual distance seems to have been introduced by Hediger, whose work on 'flight' and 'critical' distances etc. represents yet another mode of the perceptual division of space. If not belonging strictly to social life, these categories might be termed those of 'survival space'. For ethological discussions of individual distance in birds, see e.g. Conder 1949, and Crook 1961. Something like individual distance seems to be present in some primates—see e.g. Jay 1965—but it is much less neat and simple here than in birds. It is evidently an index of status among other things, rather than (as in birds) a determinant of the minimum distance between individuals in a group whose overall spacing, according to Crook, is the result of cohesive and dispersive forces.

[7] Hall 1963. cf. also Sommer's suggestion that schizophrenics have an impaired concept of personal space (Sommer 1959).

I

the European) version of individual distance; in some cases it even
brings the latter into play. Thus:

It appears that Americans, when standing face to face, stand about arm's
length from each other. When they stand side by side, the distance
demanded is much less. When 'middle majority' Americans stand closer
than this in a face-to-face position they will either gradually separate or
come toward each other and begin to emit signs of irritation. However,
if they are put in a situation in which they are not required to interact—
say on a streetcar—they can stand quite close, even to the point of
making complete contact.[1]

Of course, the physical distance itself is modified by the other
factors, such as bodily orientation, discussed by Hall under the
head of 'proxemic' systems. But it seems a reasonable guess that
in human beings and at any rate in some primates, there are
important if indirect links between 'greeting' ceremonies and the
socially relevant categories of distance—both being manipulated,
perhaps, to produce the conditions necessary for certain types of
'focussed' interaction.

   Apart from questions of distance separating individuals, there is
another way in which greeting ceremonies could be said to
'mediate' the structuring of social space. Goffman, in the following
passage, takes too simple a view of the situation he describes:

In Anglo-American society there exists a kind of 'nod line' that can be
drawn at a particular point through a rank order of communities
according to size. Any community below the line, and hence below a
certain size, will subject its adults, whether acquainted or not, to mutual
greetings; any community above this line will free all pairs of un-
acquainted persons from this obligation.[2]

This is probably true as far as it goes. But it is obvious that—
especially in the more 'urban' and 'complex' societies—many sub-
communities exist. Different channels of division and different
finenesses within a channel become perceptually prominent on
different occasions—and on different ground. One has only to
think of the different groups and sub-groups one feels a member of,
and how these and the locus of meeting would affect the greeting
offered to anyone encountered (say) on the premises of a univer-

   [1] Birdwhistell, R. 1959 in Schaffner, B. (ed.) *Group processes*, Transactions of
the 4th (1957) Conference; p. 184. Cited by Goffman 1963, p. 99 (footnote).
   [2] Goffman 1963, pp. 132–3.

sity department, in the university town, in London, abroad. We have in fact something not unlike the fission-fusion principle of segmentary lineages, where the we/they oppositions are generated by the locus of the encounter and by its degree of 'foreignness' in relation to the identifying group on which the participants base their claim to mutual recognition; and where all this is summarized in the occurrence, form and intensity of the formal acknowledgement of the meeting as a meeting—i.e. in the greeting ceremony. It is interesting to discover that something of the kind is true of the 'triumph ceremony' of geese in one of its forms—which in this context seems to be as much a demonstration of solidarity as a gesture of 'greeting'. Nevertheless, here as well we have 'fission-fusion' expressed in a rite which is closely allied to one of 'greeting':

In autumn and winter it occasionally happens that flocks of geese, consisting of several families, come back from the breeding colonies which we settled some miles away . . . Faced with these utter strangers, the otherwise mutually hostile families of geese on our lake unite in one collective phalanx of converging necks, and attempt to drive away the intruders who, in turn, form another phalanx and usually stand their ground, provided they are numerous enough.[1]

We cannot, however, link too much of human social action to the dimensions of physical space/time, even where its units are socially measured out. But it appears that our social relations themselves are often mapped on a basis of spatial metaphors of one sort or another—consider the concepts of 'social distance', 'close' and 'distant' kinship etc. One of the simplest dimensions of 'social distance' is the degree of separateness of individuals on a hierarchical scale, and it is evident (e.g. from Andrew's account) that primate 'greeting' often expresses relative social standing. In human hierarchical organizations, it is no accident that honorific modes of address ('Sir' etc.) so often cluster within the 'greeting' component of an encounter and are part of it, emphasizing the principle of classification which governs the encounter. This is also true of the more diffuse relationships of our own everyday life, where forms of address largely overlap with greeting procedures and indicate where the relationship stands on a number of related scales, of which 'closeness' provides a convenient blanket metaphor. To take an example from a modern novel:

[1] Lorenz 1966, p. 162.

Forms of address among men who work together vary. There's the 'Sir' or rank prefix by ones who don't wish to pursue their relationship, the nickname used to conceal affection or at least respect, the Christian names of friends and the surname form of address among men who think they are still at college. Only men like Ivor Butcher are called by their full name.[1]

Whether or not such relationships are spatially conceptualized in any sense, this use of greeting to structure the different degrees of acquaintanceship has its simpler parallel in horses, according to one report:

... when two horses meet for the first time, 4 stages of introduction can be clearly recognized; a) the horses circle round one another a short distance apart, b) they touch nostrils, c) each horse investigates the other's tail and body with the tip of its nose, d) if mutual tolerance is decided upon they nibble one another along the crest of the neck.[2]

There is some evidence that the 'greeting' ceremony as an instrument of classification (on a primitive basis of 'my kind'/the rest of the environment) can even operate cross-specifically in certain animals:

The decisive criterion for the occurrence of social relations between animal and man is ... the fact that individuals of a different species are included in the specific behaviour patterns of the animal ... Tigers which know each other utter a specific sound when they meet, the so-called greeting purr. In the zoo, a tame tiger will utter the same greeting signal when meeting its keeper ... In other words, man becomes subject of the tiger's specific ceremony; man is enclosed in the intra-specific behaviour; he is considered and treated as an individual of the same species.[3]

Finally, in the following ethnographic case a greeting ceremony—in the specific context of the host–guest situation—appears to 'mediate' the total structure of social relations: 'The Ibo of Eastern Nigeria conceptualize and express their lineage system, and through it map the whole of mankind ... through the idiom of the kola nut—the traditional Ibo medium of welcoming a guest and establishing ... or reinforcing ... their interaction rate.'[4]

---

[1] Deighton, Len. *Horse under water* (paperback), p. 119.
[2] Hafez et al. 1962.
[3] Hediger 1965.　　　　[4] Uchendu 1964.

What I have tried to do in this chapter is to call attention to the numerous small-scale ceremonial observances which tend to initiate encounters between individuals or small groups; and which in my view have as their common significance the 'placing' of the encounter or the relationship in social space/time and on certain other dimensions of social life—which may themselves be expressible in a spatial idiom. Examples have been drawn (admittedly they are ethnographically somewhat lopsided, but this cannot be helped) from both human and animal social life, in species where 'greeting' seemed a relevant concept—the criterion being talk of 'greeting' in the ethological literature, with or without quotation marks. I have argued that the fact of language does not in this case preclude comparison of human and animal material. Certainly it seems a remarkably neat piece of organization that meetings should be 'placed' in this way before the real business of the encounter gets going, whether it be a business negotiation or a grooming session. I wish to reserve judgement on the status of greetings with respect to signals and codes. I reject, that is, the view into which one might be tempted by reading Berne's account—that greetings are all to do with administering the right amount of social stimulation and reward, as if this excluded their being a part of communication. I believe that both human and animal greetings are properly studied at a social—i.e. a supra-individual—level; but their connection with the perceptual structuring of social relationships on the one hand, and on the other their analogies with higher-order social processes, provides further reason for re-examining the barrier between psychological and social facts.

I also reserve judgement on the precise definition of 'greeting', and whether one could be arrived at to cover both human and animal versions in a rigorous manner. What I have given throughout the chapter have been mostly rough indications of the area of social life in which 'greeting' probably lies. The evidence on animal 'greeting' is too scattered and presented in too many diverse contexts, and at present there is a real danger of distorting and misrepresenting the literature by forcing it into any rigid framework. Certainly 'greeting' is not the only kind of exchange whose significance may be as sketched above—for example aggressive encounters in which dominance is enforced may also be looked at as 'mapping' a social relationship in a similar way. Much research is needed on these—at present vaguely recognizable—mapmaking, or rather map-enacting, systems of observances. What is important in my view is that such a concept, when properly worked out and documented, should be as applicable to human social life as to that of certain other animal species.

VIII

'DOMINANCE' AND THE POSITION OF WOMEN

THE initial theme of this chapter is the position of females with respect to rank-order systems in non-human species, and whether this has any bearing on the position of women in human societies. We saw in Chapter VI that the clue to 'social control' in animals and men is to be found in the concept of 'social structure'. We saw in Chapter VII that certain small-scale rituals—notably 'greeting' in both animals and men—can be interpreted as devices which enable the structure of social relationships to be expressed and manipulated in complicated ways. I now propose to start with a predominantly structural question. Do the various 'ranking' systems, reported for a wide range of species, have a common structural core; and if so what are the consequences for all social organizations including human ones? This question need involve no prior assumptions about identities between animal and human ranking systems other than as principles of social organization. As in Chapter VII with the concept of 'greeting' I have the problem of delimiting a field in order to talk about it, without prejudging its actual unity. As before, the initial criterion is mention of 'dominance' or 'ranking' systems in the ethological literature which I have covered.

Any general treatment of the 'position' of women would be far beyond the scope of this work. Indeed one must suspect that it is for largely historical reasons that this has been marked out as an 'issue' in the first place—an issue which belongs in the political and ideological framework of women's-emancipation movements rather than that of general sociological theory. The earlier discussions of 'the position of women'—or worse, 'the status of women' —have phrased the problem (if there is one) in such a way as to turn it into a pseudo-issue for most modern readers. One certainly has the impression, reading Evans-Pritchard's essay on *The Position of Women*,[1] that he has responded in this way to the literature he

[1] Evans-Pritchard 1955.

cites; that he is somewhat at a loss for answers to questions which, for him, do not quite carry conviction. He is much happier in drawing the conclusion—undoubtedly true—that whatever we take 'position' to mean, women's position in any society depends ultimately on everybody's position.

It is particularly misleading to talk of 'status' (in the sense of high or low status) without a clear analysis of the kinds of systems in which one can have status, and this goes beyond the old-fashioned *naïveté* of describing status as 'high' or 'low' in relation to an unexpressed European middle-class norm. An example of unhelpful use of the word 'status' may be taken from Warner's *A Black Civilization*, cited and criticized by Kaberry.[1] This author believes, according to Kaberry, that the higher status (in an absolute sense) of Aboriginal men derives ultimately from their possession of a more complex technology than that of the women.[2] She quotes him as saying that among the Murngin: '... the principle of the social bifurcation of the sexes has been used to create the lowest status, that of women and children.'[3] Kaberry's quarrel is principally with Warner's view of male sanctity (and hence 'high status') as opposed to female profaneness (and hence 'low status'). But from her overall account it is clear that the concept of 'status' contributes nothing to the ethnography of Aboriginal women. It neglects the real flexibility of the system; worse, it misrepresents the complex relationship between the sexes, which is many-fronted, and cannot in principle be summarized on a unidimensional model. The idea of 'status', where it invokes an opposition of 'higher' to 'lower', presupposes the idea of a scale of some sort, even if it is only a two-step one.[4] And it cannot be a simple matter to discover, at the level of human societies, what are the scales and principles on which 'status' is allotted—be it the 'status' of a woman *vis-à-vis* men, other women or anybody. Thurnwald[5] reports that in Buin society the daughters and principal wives of chiefs, despite their 'privileged position', work as hard as other women and at the same tasks; nor do they command any greater deference from the men than do other women. Distinctions of this kind must precede any blanket judgment of the

---

[1] Kaberry 1939.   [2] ibid., p. 164.   [3] ibid., p. 220.
[4] This is not to deny that 'status' can be used in a non-hierarchical sense, as by Beattie in *Other Cultures*.
[5] Thurnwald 1934.

'status of women' in societies—and will in most cases super-annuate such judgements. The only contexts where 'status' in this sense is of much relevance to a discussion of the position of women are (as Evans-Pritchard says) where inequalities of degree rather than of kind are purposely built in as premises of the social system —as where the bloodmoney for a woman is less than that payable for a man. But it can still be asked how far this situation influences the immediate realities of social life. None of this is particularly controversial. It is intended simply to rule out from the start any idea that one could proceed from ethological comparisons to 'explain' the 'status of women' in human societies, as if it were clear in advance what this meant.

How much, then, can we expect of ethological comparisons in the context of women's position in human societies? Evans-Pritchard has written that "The facts seem . . . to suggest that there are deep biological and psychological factors, as well as sociological factors, involved, and that the relation between the sexes can only be modified by social changes, and not radically altered by them.'[1] It will be apparent by now that I am not happy about contrasting these 'biological' and 'sociological' factors, although I do not wish, like some authors, to take the latter as a simple sub-case of the former.[2] I think rather that the concept of 'sociological factors' ought to be widened so as to allow us to speak of social facts, social processes and social structures, without quotation marks, in a number of non-human contexts where traditional biological accounts in terms of function and survival value also apply. Thus there is no intrinsic opposition between 'biological' and 'sociological' thinking; yet to say so is not to open the door to simplistic biological 'explanations' of human social events in the all-revealing tone of voice which some ethologists are prone to adopt. It seems to me that a study of the part that females play in different kinds of non-human social organization provides a good area for examining two of the possible relevancies of ethology to social anthropology; (a) the prospect of discovering that *being the species we are*, we are committed to a particular range of social systems (this might be a

[1] Evans-Pritchard 1955.
[2] I also believe that what many psychologists regard as 'psychological factors' are based on a very uneasy and doubtful amalgam of the biological and the societal. Cf. Argyle 1967, p. 13: 'In the present state of knowledge it looks as if social behaviour is the result of at least seven different drives . . .'

kind of taxonomic determinism) and (b) an analysis of the logical possibilities inherent in social organizations—an analysis more wide-ranging than could be achieved by considering existing human societies alone; and for this reason, perhaps, likely to suggest more abstract and fundamental principles underlying social systems. One discovery which might ultimately be made (though not on the evidence I have managed to collect) is that the various societal definitions of women can be regarded as attempts to resolve a primitive structural problem which *Homo sapiens* shares with other socially organized species.

ETHOLOGICAL EVIDENCE

(a) *The range of possibilities.* Several ethological writers have hinted in rather a vague manner that non-human social organizations based on rank-order systems, and those based on rights over property and space, represent structural alternatives of some kind. The either/or is evidently of the inclusive sort, allowing for combinations and compromises (cf. Leyhausen's account[1] of shifting 'relative' and 'absolute' dominance in cats according to the amount of space available for the local habitation of individuals). Wynne-Edwards writes: 'As a general rule . . . social competition is directed towards these dual and essential prizes—social status on the one hand, and a claim or tenure of property on the other. Depending on the particular type of social organization, one of these goals may often appear to eclipse the other.'[2] This must be evaluated in the context of his view of conventional competition (see Chapter v). Ardrey claims that for primates 'An effective social organization . . . will be achieved through territory, or it will be achieved through tyranny. Contemporary research has revealed no third way.'[3] But for a criticism of Ardrey's documentation, see subsection (b) below. Imanishi makes a related point: '. . . there are at least two distinct patterns of organization at the *oikia* level. In the one pattern, each *oikia* has its own territory and is antagonistic to contiguous *oikiae*, though it may accept a solitary intruder in some cases. In the other pattern, each *oikia* associates easily with contiguous *oikiae* under normal circumstances, the *oikiae* together

---

[1] Leyhausen 1965.
[2] Wynne-Edwards 1962, p. 134.
[3] Ardrey 1967, p. 219.

forming a large band or troop.'[1] It is not clear how general his remarks are intended to be; although the concept of the *oikia* is certainly intended to apply throughout the animal kingdom. It will be seen that Ardrey's 'no third way' is not consistent with Imanishi's 'at least'; nor has the idea been set out, to my knowldge, as a systematic hypothesis. But it is worth being aware of the possibility that 'rank' and 'property' (including territory) in animals represent alternative structural principles of a primitive kind. We have seen in Chapter 6 that they may represent alternative systems of social control on aggression, by imposing regularity on the occurrence and evasion of agonistic encounters. This provides a context for enquiring whether the former type of organization presents any peculiar problems for the 'placing' of the females within it.

It is impossible to give a simple definition of 'dominance' relationships, valid for every species in which they are said to occur. This is partly because of the different techniques of observation and analysis appropriate to different animal groups. Schelderup-Ebbe's simple conception of the peck-order can be worked out in chickens or pigeons by counting up the number of attacks every bird makes and receives from every other, or by setting up very simple competitive situations between pairs of individuals. This method alone could not accurately reflect the subtleties of ranking systems at the primate level, although the frequency and outcome of aggressive encounters clearly has something to do with 'dominance' in non-human primates. Thus de Vore and Hall,[2] writing of baboon social behaviour, say that in one small group the dominant males (a) mated most frequently with full-grown females, (b) were 'presented' to most frequently, (c) 'took the lead' in disturbing situations, (d) were involved in the largest number of aggressive episodes, (c) attracted 'clusters' of females with newborn young. It is hard to say whether any of these could be taken as a decisive criterion of 'dominance' in baboons. The method of placing food between pairs of individuals to determine the 'dominance' relation between them, has been used with, for example, bonnet macaques[3]—but this too would seem a little crude if not confirmed by other regularities in the animals' behaviour to one

---

[1] Imanishi 1960. An *oikia* is 'the minimum unit of social life found in any species of animal, regardless of the composition of that unit.'
[2] De Vore & Hall 1965.   [3] See Simonds 1965.

another. Therefore we cannot automatically take 'dominance' to be in its own right an adequate unifying concept for the different animal social systems in which it is described. It has recently been suggested, indeed,[1] that the whole concept of 'dominance' at the primate level ought to be replaced by a finer analysis of the structuring of mutual attention within more or less cohesive groups. With these reservations, however, it is possible to say that a number of animal species have in common a social organization based on relative status (loosely defined) in at least one sex, and that this involves, roughly, differentials of access to certain resources. The term 'status' belongs in quotation marks and evokes no pseudo-human idea of 'leadership'.[2] I shall accordingly speak of 'status' in this loose sense, to denote whatever may be common to these social systems based on relative rank (leaving out, for the moment, the human case), although 'dominance' and 'rank-order' in the literature often have a stronger and more specific meaning. I assumed at the beginning of Chapter VII that 'greeting' in non-human contexts was a single class of behaviour. I shall make a corresponding assumption here—that something of a comparable kind is happening in 'hierarchical' organizations in widely separate groups—organizations which, on a Darwinian sexual-selection or a Wynne-Edwards population-control theory, would be taken as functionally equivalent to one another. The object of immediate concern is the forms that these 'status' organizations can take, and the theoretical possibilities for the relationship between the sexes on a 'status' framework.

One broad feature of the ethological literature on 'dominance' is that competition for status is predominantly a male concern. There are of course counter-examples such as chickens and cows, and 'harem' systems generally. Here, the female groups may exhibit fairly typical rank-order relations, while 'status' among the males is measured by the number of females they can hold on to in the face of competition from rivals. It may be significant that chickens and cows, for example, are domesticated species which

---

[1] Chance 1967.

[2] If it is justifiable to speak of 'leadership' in animal groups, as for example it might be in female herds of red deer, then 'leadership', although it might coincide with 'status', means something rather different from it. Thompson (1958) implicitly contrasts 'leadership' among female red deer with 'dominance' among the males. 'Status' in animals is, however, linked in a number of ways with social control—see Chapter VI.

often live in all-female communities, and this may have had the effect of exaggerating rank differentials between females. Grant and Chance,[1] studying rank-order in caged rats, worked predominantly with males but did observe relatively unstable rank-orders in all-female groups. They do not report what happens in mixed groups. We can guess that even where ranking is primarily a male affair, females are often potentially able to 'take over' under certain conditions, and a completely independent female hierarchy is one possible solution to the problem of placing females in social organizations based on differentials of rank between males. But we may suspect that—apart from the harem situation—it is at best a short-term arrangement of limited scope, or else an adaptation to abnormal conditions, whether we are dealing with single-sex groups of domestic animals or with hierarchical girls' or women's organizations in our own society.

The structural problem presented by male rank-order systems is most evident, perhaps, in some birds. Any but the briefest co-operative relation between the sexes—e.g. in defence of a nesting-site or territory —means that the female must somehow be accommodated to the rank of her mate *vis-à-vis* other males, since she is directly concerned in most of his aggressive and competitive encounters. It is theoretically possible, perhaps, for males and females of a group to strive independently for status in competition with one another, but this will clearly be wasteful and inefficient if the system also demands prolonged co-operation between mates of a pair. (It is frequently true, on the other hand, that within a pair the male regularly outranks the female—but 'rank' here may not mean quite the same thing; see below). Wynne-Edwards cites the black-crowned night-heron as an example of a species where individuals seem to be ranked irrespective of sex; but he suspects that such an organization '. . . is in effect asexual, and concerns a group of neuter individuals in which there are no established pairs and no interest in reproduction.'[2] Another possibility is that the females remain completely outside the rank-order competition of the males; nor do they stand in any such relation to one another. This again seems to presuppose the absence of pair-bonding or any lasting relationship between individuals of opposite sex, and hence of co-operation in rearing the young. This seems to be the case with 'arena' species of birds; there is some evidence that it is also

[1] Grant and Chance 1958.   [2] Wynne-Edwards 1962, p. 156.

true of dolphins.[1] The problem seems to arise, at any rate for birds, where the differential ranking of males as a governing principle of social organization coincides with an economic need for lasting co-operation between individuals of a pair. Great tits show one way of resolving this, according to Brian's observations.[2] Here, relative dominance was measured by priority of access to a food-source. The male and female dominance orders were found to be distinct, but 'complementary in that the members of a pair occupied corresponding positions, the one in the male and the other in the female order.' It was however impossible to tell for certain whether the status of the females was dependent on that of their mates, since relative dominance was largely a function of the distance between the feeding place and the bird's territory. A more complete integration of the female into the male ranking system, is seen in jackdaws (*Corvus monedula*)[3]. In this species, the males and females of a colony apparently participate individually in a common status hierarchy until they form pairs, whereupon the female assumes the rank of her mate. This generally involves a promotion; and the female thereafter threatens not only subordinate females but subordinate males as well. Lorenz[4] reports a similar system in tame but free-flying greylag geese (*Anser anser*); but Boyd has commented that this concept of rank belongs to relatively small closed groups and does not apply to, for example, wild white-fronted geese in winter flocks.

Thus given closed groups organized around rank-order systems among males, there are a number of logical alternatives with respect to the females. Five of these possibilities have been outlined above; (a) complete non-participation by the females in any 'ranking' behaviour; (b) independent hierarchies among the females irrespective of the males; (c) indiscriminate competition for rank by both sexes within a single system; (d) a separate rank-order among the females, associated in some way with that of the males; (e) the assimilation of the mated female to the rank of her mate, whereby she becomes his equivalent in rank-order confrontations, although a 'dominance' relation may exist between them. In (b)

---

[1] See McBride, Arthur & Hebb 1948.   [2] Brian 1949.
[3] Lorenz 1952; *King Solomon's Ring* and 1935, 'Der Kumpan in der Umwelt des Vogels'; reprinted 1957 in Schiller (ed.) *Instinctive Behaviour*, pp. 83–116. Cited by Brian 1949; these observations were unfortunately cut from the English translation.
[4] Lorenz 1935 ibid.; cited by Boyd 1953.

and (d) the females are, structurally speaking, in competition with one another only; in (c) and (e) they are in competition with all other members of the group.

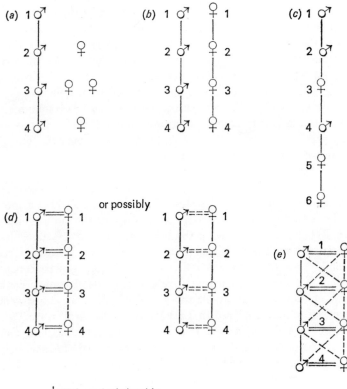

|='Primary' relationship
╎='Derived' relationship
===relatively long term association -not necessarily one-to-one
  -between individuals of opposite sex.
Vertical dimension denotes relative 'rank'.

Fig. I

Each of these sketches represents the barest bones of a system; even at the level of birds, a number of other factors intrude and make a comparative discussion difficult. There is also the difficulty, parallel to that discussed in Chapter VI (p. 83), of treating relative status among males as 'primary' to the system and other things as flowing from it. It seems likely, however, that the choice of system turns largely on the type and extent of co-operation between the sexes. In particular, of the five schemes listed above, only the last two appear to be compatible with lasting (including seasonal) pair-bonds and with prolonged co-operation between mates in defending the 'home' and rearing the young. We may guess that this question of prolonged and close co-operation between individuals[1] sets a general limit to the variability of any dominance-based social organization.

A somewhat different question is that of the rank-order relationship, if any, existing between actual or potential sexual partners. I suggested above that one should distinguish between 'rank' in the context of—say—the competing males of a social group, and in that of the sexual relationship between individuals. It is said of many species that the male is regularly 'dominant' over the female, whether in a true 'pair-bond' situation or a short-term 'consort' relationship.[2] There is also the apparently close evolutionary connection, particularly at primate level, between 'submission' as a social and as a purely sexual gesture. This was discussed in Chapter VII. Thus 'submissive' behaviour may look much the same in either case. But the logical bases of the two patterns may be somewhat different. In the case of sexual partners, it looks as if the difference of 'rank' between them may reflect the combination of tendencies in each without which a sexual relationship itself cannot come about. This can be most plausibly said of animals whose social behaviour can be analysed in a relatively 'mechanical' way. Thus Oehlert[3] has demonstrated that in two species of cichlid fish, sexual recognition, and therefore heterosexual pair formation, is made possible by the fact that sexual arousal in males can combine only with aggressive, in females only with flight, motivation. It follows that in any question of rank-order between established partners the male will be dominant. But similarly, in the infinitely more complex social organization of rhesus monkeys, (which do not form lasting pair-bonds) Harlow[4] reports that 'females show no respect for a male they can dominate . . .' and hence, presum-

---

[1] Co-operation, that is, which involves attentive interaction between partners, and not in the merely functional sense whereby, for example, the presence of an aggressive male would bring general protection to females and young.

[2] See e.g. Lorenz 1966, p. 106 on emerald lizards; Brian 1949 on great tits; Carpenter 1942 on rhesus monkeys.

[3] Oehlert 1958. Kampf und Paarbildung einiger Cichliden. *Zeitschrift für Tierpsychologie*, 15, 141–74. Cited by Hess 1962.

[4] Harlow 1962.

ably, will not consort with him. There seems to be no good reason for avoiding the terms 'dominance' and 'rank' in relation to actual or prospective sexual partners, provided one recognizes that the basis of this, both structurally and functionally, may be rather different from that of other systems based on relative status. A crucial question, which cannot be analysed here, concerns the nature of the competitive situation underlying both kinds of 'dominance'.

(b) *The primate picture*. Chance claimed in 1960 that 'The essential characteristic of a primate society is that members of both sexes live together within the structure created by a male dominance order which may cause a breakup into 'family' groups, or groups with other special characteristics.'[1] Later field-studies showed that this is not true of every primate species, but in some at least we are clearly dealing with social organizations based on differentials of 'rank' between males. In 1963 he enlarged this view, which is still, clearly, to be taken as a very general summary:

I am far from dismissing the bond between the females of non-human primates, which may possess a weak motivational component similar to that of the males, but which is at present unexplained. Nevertheless, their behaviour differs in important respects from that of the males in three ways. Firstly, it is less structured and secondly, they are grouped round the male or the male hierarchy and thirdly, there are strong attractive influences present bringing them together because of the presence of young.[2]

This kind of thinking has largely replaced the older view—held for example by Zuckerman—that crude sexuality is 'the only enduring basis' of primate social life, and that 'the nucleus of societies of monkeys and apes is the family party, consisting of an overlord and his harem, held together primarily by the interest of the male in his females and by their interest in their young.'[3]

It is at this level of generality that the primate studies are of most interest in the present context; certainly it would be a mistake to dig too deeply into the literature on primate dominance without being qualified to assess it in detail. But at least one distinction ought to be made, parallel to that discussed above, between 'dominance' as a system whereby individuals of a group possess unequal rights to such resources as food, space or sexual partners,

---

[1] Chance 1960. Comment on Imanishi 1960. [2] Chance 1963.
[3] Imanishi 1960 (who rejects this view).

and as a regular precondition of the sexual relationship itself. It is the latter which Ardrey seems to mean when he compares the position of the primate female in 'tyrannical' and 'territorial' settings in order to illustrate his view of "Territory and a voluntary association of partners for whom equal siege brings closer equality of status, and with it something resembling the personal dignity which man so prizes.'[1] But it is difficult to attach much meaning to Ardrey's language of 'freedom' and 'oppressiveness' in primate society. It may be true that the female member of a patas harem receives fewer threats from the male than her hamadryas counterpart, but in what sense can she 'choose' not to behave as she does? Moreover, no obvious connection between territoriality and peacefulness within the group seems to follow from Ardrey's cited sources on hamadryas and patas groups.[2] The paper of Hall and his colleagues concerns a small laboratory group of patas monkeys, and is basically an inventory of their repertoire of gestures and sounds. The authors do say that patas lack conspicuous 'dominant' and 'submissive' patterns of behaviour and that in the wild, aggressive behaviour within one-male groups is rare, but they do not relate this explicitly to territorial defence. It is doubtful, too, whether the one-male groups of Ethiopian hamadryas baboons and patas monkeys present a test case, as Ardrey implies, for they differ in another respect than simple territoriality. The hamadryas groups exist within a larger troop whose overall composition is loose and unstable; hence it can be argued that a greater amount of selective attention and sheer 'fuss' is required to keep these minimal units together. For a true test case to prove or disprove Ardrey's contention that territory alone brings internal harmony, we would have to find a species of monkey which is both nonterritorial and lives in genuinely isolated one-male groups. In any case Kummer's analysis[3] of the structure of dependent, protective and aggressive behaviour within the one-male hamadryas group is clearly more helpful than Ardrey's talk of 'abuse' of the female.[4]

I have not come across any other attempts to correlate the position of the females in primate society with simple variables in their

---

[1] Ardrey 1966, p. 255.

[2] Kummer and Kurt 1963. Hall, Boelkins and Goswell 1965.

[3] Kummer 1968.

[4] Cf. also Hall's view that dominance in Chacma baboons is expressed in their protectiveness towards females with nursing infants as 'nuclear' animals of the group. (Hall 1963.)

ecology or social organization, although the possibility of such a correlation, presumably, remains open. What does seem to be true is that in species where the relationship between the males of a group is strongly hierarchical, the position of the females is equivocal with respect to that hierarchy. This applies predominantly to the monkeys rather than to the apes, and in making this point I rely heavily on Chance's[1] summary, which admittedly predates many of the most important field studies. Chance takes this central hierarchy of males (in, for example, Japanese and Indian macaques, hamadryas baboons, South American howler and spider monkeys) as a starting point for analysing the relationships between other categories of group members; if he is right, therefore, the position of females in relation to male ranking systems is a thoroughly meaningful issue in primate studies.

The rhesus macaque (*Macaca mulatta*) presents a well-documented case where the shifting character of the female's social position seems to be a function of the oestral cycle and the pattern of temporary consort relationships with males of the central hierarchy. Carpenter[2] reported that 'The increased aggressiveness of the female (during oestrus) results in her ascending in the female dominance scale . . . and often, with the reinforcement of her male consort, she becomes temporarily the most dominant of all the females in her group and, in addition, she may occupy the most preferred place of safety in the most dominant male's sphere of protection.' Carpenter's further comment that oestrus 'both motivates non-conformist behaviour and makes it possible at the same time for females to cross group boundaries' suggests that the oestral cycle in rhesus females is, among other things, an anti-reactionary device, ensuring that relations among the female group at least are periodically brought under revision.[3]

Broadly speaking, then, the position of the female in terms of 'rank' is a contingent and relative one. On the other hand, possibly in this species and certainly in the Japanese macaque (*M. fuscata*) the females as a category occupy a crucial position in relation to the diachronic structure of the group. Fig. II is adapted from Imanishi.[4]

[1] Chance 1963.   [2] Carpenter 1942.
[3] Cf. Carpenter 1965, p. 289, on howler monkeys: 'The rotational consort pattern . . . is a positive conditioning in which the oestrous female periodically reinforces interactions with the adult males of the group'.
[4] Imanishi 1960.

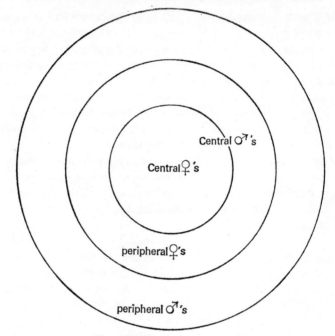

FIG. II (after Imanishi 1960)

As the mother–infant tie loosens the juvenile males are forced out to the 'periphery' of the group; from here, as they mature and in competition with one another, they work their way back into the central dominant core. But since relative dominance among the adult females is linked to the closeness of their relationship with the dominant males, the sons of these dominant females start off with a built-in advantage in the competition for rank, since they in turn are most readily recognized and tolerated by the central males. This advantage is even greater for females whose mothers are dominant, since they are never shifted out to the periphery. Imanishi quotes Kawai's earlier distinction between 'basic' and 'dependent' rank, especially among juveniles: '. . . the basic rank among [juvenile] males is recognized during and after peripheriza-tion . . . Females, in contrast, remain in the central part from birth to death, so that they constantly grow under the influence of dependent-rank effect, and this, in turn, induces among them a solidification of dependent rank into basic rank.'[1] Etkin[2] speaks of

[1] Imanishi 1960.   [2] Etkin 1964.

this system as 'adumbrating' social class structure—a suitably non-committal word. Certainly the idea of 'basic' and 'dependent' rank is very close to the distinction which a number of social anthropologists have made, between 'ascribed' and 'achieved' status, not least in the fact that in many cases the 'ascription' of status is not absolute nor unchallengeable. That is, it confers a holder's advantage but is often provisional in nature, requiring to be 'solidified' by the exercise of individual ability. What is even more interesting is that although, as Chance says, Japanese macaque groups are conspicuously organized round the hierarchy of dominant males, an individual's position in the community is largely a function of his or her links with a particular female. The females, in a sense, form the structural hub of the system.

Thus a general feature of primate systems, at least among the monkeys where male dominance orders are strongly marked, seems to be that relationships among the females are relatively un-organized and un-structured. This may partly reflect the disruptive influence of oestrus—as in rhesus macaques—but this in turn seems to work by altering the pattern of male–female relations from which those among the females apparently follow. Chance cites Itani's observations of Japanese macaques:

...he has not called this gathering of females a group and there is a reason; they lack the social organization and the social relations which are characteristic of each of the other groups—the dominant males, the sub-dominant males and the sub-adult males. The grouping of the females is the most noisy and undisciplined of all the associations. There is no clear recognition of dominance . . . for instance a female of lower rank may very well attack a female of higher rank by placing herself under the protection of one of the dominant males . . . Here we see how much more clearly they are oriented to the males than to themselves.[1]

We have seen that this situation may be paralleled in other animals —for example, in rats.[2] It would be convenient if one could apply to primate groups the kind of typology sketched in Fig. I. Unfortunately, the evidence does not permit this. One may guess, for example, that the macaque systems are variants of type (d) above, with (in the case of *M. mulatta*) the rank of the female shifting with her consort associations and ultimately with her oestral state. But

[1] Chance 1963. Cf. also Jay 1965 and Schaller 1965.
[2] Grant and Chance 1958.

it is not to my knowledge made clear, either for *mulatta* or *fuscata*, precisely how the rank of the female follows from her association with a particular male—or whether indeed the rank comes before the association.[1]

The other side of this particular coin is, as I have suggested, the position of the females of at least one primate species as conveyors of rank and perpetuators of the system, even where their own rank is equivocal. This may come about through processes of individual teaching and learning which are not of directly sociological concern. An interesting parallel might be found here with Margaret Mead's picture of the American mother of the 1940s as definer of the elements of success and achievement, in a system where direct participation is reserved implicitly for men.[2]

As the literature stands at present this is, I believe, about as far as one can go, both in analysing the position of females in dominance-based primate societies and in 'structuralizing' on this topic as an experimental exercise. We must turn now to questions about the relevance of such a discussion to the investigation of human societies and society.

CONSEQUENCES AND RELATED ISSUES

The foregoing discussion was concerned with ways in which, in animal societies, males and females as categories within a group contribute to its 'structure' in a primitive sense. Such a molar approach would not take one very far towards an anthropological understanding of human society as a whole, or women's position in it. Ethologists tend to recommend that we find out which elements of human behaviour are 'archaic' or 'instinctive', in order to discover what limits are set to 'cultural' elaboration; but in this case at least the evidence does not seem to warrant much speculation of this kind. That is to say, I do not think it is worth making great efforts to guess whether rank-order relationships (however defined) are intrinsic to human social life as a species-specific trait, as they are intrinsic to the social life of (say) macaques. There is, indeed, room for doubt whether this question is itself very meaningful. But the ethological evidence suggests, I think, that

---

[1] But see the observations of 'protected threat' among female primates. See e.g. Hall & De Vore 1965, esp. p. 65.
[2] Mead 1949: esp. Chapter XV.

differential rank is one of (perhaps) several principles on a basis of which, more or less comprehensively, 'social control' can come about and a society can be organized. If then we consider ranking systems as structural principles rather than as unalterable sequences of inherited behaviour (which they may be in addition) it becomes possible to look for features common to hierarchical systems where they occur in human and animal social organizations, without having to answer in advance questions about what mankind is genetically committed to. We are looking in the direction, not of a statement of the form 'The robin is/is not a pair-forming terri- torial species', with 'man' substituted for 'the robin'; but rather of some fulfilment of Etkin's proposition that 'Progress . . . depends, not upon reliance on occasional analogies, but upon recognizing the vast variety of forms that the same fundamental principles can take in the kaleidoscope of nature.'[1]

With this as background it is possible to consider human hierarchies as having structural affinities with 'dominance' systems in animals, whatever the scope of influence of such hierarchies in the societies where they occur. We do not have the problem of selecting units of comparable range to bring together in the first place, as we should if we tried misguidedly to compare, say, the dominance-based social organization of an animal species with a particular tribe or community whose institutions seemed to be strongly hierarchical. But it is rapidly becoming less and less clear exactly what in human social systems might be comparable to the kind of structural sketches I attempted earlier, in which females' relationships with one another and with males are seen as following out certain possibilities 'given' in the nature of the hierarchical relation between the males which forms the supporting centre of the system. When we come to consider what anthropological insights are derivable from this viewpoint, it is less a question of pointing with a triumphant cry to actual examples which fit the picture, than of urging that more work be done by ethnographers and theoreticians on the nature of 'status' and of competition for status, and how this may be expected to affect men and women differentially in different social settings. Whether or not a biologi- cal view of rank is going to be ultimately useful in this context simply cannot be decided yet. Its usefulness certainly cannot be a built-in article of faith at this stage.

[1] Etkin 1964.

An example of the kind of analysis which, I believe, could profitably be extended on the above lines, is La Fontaine's study of murder and suicide among the Gisu. Discussing specifically the kinds of failure which may lead men and women of this society to commit suicide for different reasons, this author writes

There is . . . a potent source of conflict in the fact that husband and wife both utilize the same resources, but with different ends in view. She is primarily concerned with getting the best she can for her children; his aim is to use his economic resources to improve his own status in the society.

. . . As far as Gisu are concerned . . . the point is not that women have a lower status than men but that their status is based on a different scale of values. They do not enter into competition for prestige as men do. Consequently, they are less sensitive to changes in the economic state of the society and in old age do not suffer the isolation which inability to compete for power imposes on old men.

. . . Women have lower status than men. However, this lower status does not really fit into the male status hierarchy; it is defined by other non-competitive criteria . . . it is the involvement of individuals in a competitive status hierarchy rather than the fact of relative status in a hierarchy that is a factor in the situation.[1]

There are difficulties, then, about any attempt to find exact counterparts in human society to the patterns discussed above. Despite all attempts to stick to a 'purely' structural level of analysis, it is difficult to be sure that one has not illicitly smuggled in prior assumptions about the actual relationship between animal ranking systems and human hierarchical institutions. I suggest that, on the contrary, the aim should be to work towards a 'minimal' definition of 'rank' as such, very probably incorporating a biological view among others, which would reveal where the structural identities lie between human and animal cases and what their consequences are over the whole range of social organization. To achieve this, research must proceed in parallel over the various fields concerned; and if assumptions are made which are not quite warranted by the progress of conceptual analysis, one can at least be aware that they are being made. It would be a mistake, too, to regard the conceptual framework of ethological studies as wholly fixed (although as I have said elsewhere (p. 33) ethology is less fluid theoretically than is social anthropology). It is not the case that we are looking

[1] La Fontaine 1960.

for a view of 'status' and the position of women in human societies which can be accommodated to an ethological definition of 'rank', not itself subject to revision. This is, one may suspect, an area where ethologists themselves have been insufficiently critical of their own assumptions—assumptions which may underlie the introduction, as technical terms, of words such as 'dominance', 'status' or more obviously 'leadership'. (It should be said that such a criticism applies more to the recent studies of 'higher' mammals than to the classical investigations performed by the Tinbergen school. But this may be partly because the carefully controlled phylogeny/ontogeny/survival-value matrix of the latter could seem relatively barren to someone trying to make sense of the more complicated social life of these 'higher' species. Clearly it would be not a bad thing to try to develop a more sophisticated idea of social facts in both human and animal fields, in the hope of bridging this particular gap.) This at any rate is the approach of M. R. A. Chance, who wishes to see more emphasis on systems of behaviour regarded as possessing structure and internal logic of their own, and feels that this should precede definitions in purely functional terms.

This partly re-phrases the classical insistence on detailed and accurate reporting of behaviour, but it also represents a real departure, for it introduces the possibility of a structural level of analysis of social organization in animals, which could ultimately match up with the structural approach in anthropology. As far as the present topic is concerned, it seems likely that traditional concepts of 'dominance' in animals, at primate level at least, will have to be revised in the light of Chance's work on the structure of attention.[1] Chance wants to take the analysis of primate rank-orders further back than the mere concept of 'dominance', and to consider how differential rank comes about through the structuring of the attention each group member pays to others on different occasions. He suggests that a similar mechanism governs the dominance orders of other species as well. This leaves the field wide open for investigating the position of females in relation to male ranking systems—although it does not, I think, invalidate the kind of structural mapping attempted in Fig. I. Such a general reconsideration provides us, in the human case, with a certain welcome latitude in deciding what cases are to count as comparable,

[1] Chance 1967.

from this same structural point of view. Thus it will not be necessary to confine attention to unmistakably 'hierarchical' institutions in human societies—although it should come as no surprise if, as seems often to be the case in our own European middle-class society, attempts to assimilate women to traditionally male hierarchical systems after pattern (c) (Fig. I) meet with a certain awkwardness and difficulty.[1]

But to throw the field open in this way is to sacrifice much of the apparent clarity of the question. Up to now in this chapter, we have been taking 'rank' in some sense as central to our analysis, despite misgivings about the comparability of 'rank-orders' in remotely related species. It may be, however, that the idea of 'rank-order' is itself too limited for what we are really dealing with. I should like to suggest, roughly, that one structural feature common to a good deal of human and animal social life is that the males are the conspicuous participators, the upholders of the contours and corners of the social map, and that the position of the female is characteristically more subtle or even equivocal with respect to this map. This may come about in evolution for quite simple reasons connected with the relative degrees of 'biological expendability' of male and female, particularly in species where the young are slow to develop and/or child-rearing is predominantly the concern of the female. The male is then released for the activity of maintaining a social structure, and presumably the advantages of having such a structure are sufficient to justify subjecting the male (once his essential function of fertilization is accomplished) to the increased hazard of conspicuous appearance or behaviour associated with social competition. This idea of 'conspicuous participation' is admittedly a loose one, and must remain so at this stage. One or two examples will perhaps suggest the kinds of meaning it might carry in a human social context.

Goffman, writing of present-day Anglo-American society, notes the following:

some evidence suggests that women, in general, are more tightly defined than men . . . and yet, of course, women are sometimes defined as

---

[1] Such a remark is of course pretty empty without more detailed discussion of the links between 'status', 'authority' and 'achievement' in a given social setting, and what it means to compete for them. Margaret Mead's *Male and Female* (1949) contains as good an analysis as any of this problem in the context of American society.

creatures who are not expected to be full-fledged participants in public meetings, and so can sometimes engage in somewhat taxing side involvements such as knitting, in recognition that they have not been drawn into the occasioned main involvement.[1]

An almost exact illustration of this is to be found in D. H. Lawrence's *Lady Chatterley's Lover*. Sir Clifford Chatterley spends long evenings with his friends talking about 'the life of the mind'; his wife Connie sits patiently on the edge of the group with her sewing. She is expected to be present, but not to participate directly:

Silence fell. The four men smoked. And Connie sat there and put another stitch in her sewing . . . Yes, she sat there! She had to sit mum. She had to be as quiet as a mouse, not to interfere with the immensely important speculations of these highly-mental gentlemen. But she had to be there. They didn't get on so well without her; their ideas didn't flow so freely.

. . . 'There are nice women in the world,' said Connie, lifting up her head and speaking at last.

The men resented it . . . she should have pretended to hear nothing. They hated her admitting that she had attended so closely to such talk.[2]

But if the males are characteristically the performing executives in social transactions, it looks as if females often are, in some way as yet thoroughly obscure, the keepers-in-being of the system as a system; the maintainers and perpetuators of its shape. Imanishi's findings on Japanese macaques have already been cited. In quite another way, the aspirations of Chaucer's burgesses' wives find echoes, of a conversational kind at least:

> Everich, for the wisdom that he kan,
> Was shaply for to been an alderman;
> For cattel hadde they ynough, and rente
> And eek hir wyves wolde it well assente,
> And elles certeyn were they to blame.
> It is full fair to be ycleped Madame,
> And goon to viligies al bifore,
> And have a mantel roialliche ybore.[3]

It is interesting also to compare the game of 'Let's You and Him Fight', played typically by a woman and two men and identified

[1] Goffman 1963, pp. 204–5.
[2] D. H. Lawrence. *Lady Chatterley's Lover*. Penguin edn., pp. 36–7; 42.
[3] Chaucer: Prologue to *The Canterbury Tales*.

by Berne[1] as a focus of much imaginative art, with Lorenz's work on 'incitement' by the females of certain species of swimming ducks.[2] These females, it appears, actively provoke fights between their mates and neighbouring males, thereby presumably reinforcing the map (in this case territorial) of social relations. In some species the 'inciting' procedure has been transformed into a 'ritualized' component of courtship behaviour, but Lorenz reports that in ruddy sheldrakes and Egyptian geese 'inciting really deserves its name, for the males react like fierce dogs that only await their master's signal to release their fury. In these species the function of inciting is intimately connected with that of territorial defence. Heinroth found that the males could agree in a communal enclosure if all the females were removed.'[3]

The question of non-aggression towards females is clearly relevant to their position in relation to systems dominated by competitiveness among males, but it is not discussed here because there appears to be little evidence on how the immunity of females from attack correlates with other features of social organization.[4] Non-aggression towards females is certainly not a universal feature of animal social organizations, and one could find numerous examples of human societies where women are emphatically not immune from deliberate attack in warfare. For example Thurnwald says of Buin society that:

In the old times, married life was often cut short by feuds and wars in which women and children were not spared.[5]

This idea of 'conspicuous participation', I feel, could be substituted for 'rank-order' in Figure I, in the primate material and in the human case as well. 'Rank-order' would then become a subcase of what we are talking about. As far as the non-human primates are concerned, this would accord well with recent thinking such as Chance's on the concept of 'dominance' in ethology. It is

[1] Berne 1966.
[2] Cited by Hess 1962. The main point of this research was to demonstrate by comparative analysis, the progressive stages of 'ritualization' of a piece of behaviour.
[3] Lorenz 1966, pp. 52–3.
[4] But see W. M. S. Russell's view (1968) that victimization of females and young is, in a number of species including our own, a specific response to increase in the pressure of population on resources such as food and living space.
[5] Thurnwald 1934.

worth considering whether a built-in ambiguity and looseness in the position of females is yet another way of resolving the problem of what to do with them in a system dominated by male participation—and hence belongs under a new heading in Figure I.

At this point we come very close to an argument of Mary Douglas' about the position of women (*Purity and Danger*, Chapter IX.) Dr. Douglas believes that societies in which pollution anxieties centre on sex are likely to be those where male status is defined in terms of rights over women, and where the principle of male dominance conflicts with the reality of women's capacity for manoeuvring and intrigue. She is interested in the qualities of women as individuals which give them power to sabotage the system—unless, as she says, male dominance is uncompromisingly enforced. I should like to see more attention given to the properties of females (whether human or not) as a category within a system. If it is feasible to regard a 'deliberate' looseness in the position of females as belonging under a new head in Figure I, and as a pattern which the primates have made peculiarly their own, then I suggest that human societies in turn have added their ingenious twist. There are instances, it seems, where the equivocal placing of women in situations of actual or potential conflict between men, can turn them into agents of social control. This can evidently happen whether or not the women themselves are at risk, as the following examples will show.

Kaberry's picture of the rôle of Aboriginal women in quarrels between men demonstrates rather nicely their dual position as eggers-on of (status-determining?) conflict, and as, probably, the only people who can keep fighting within bounds without anyone losing face in the process:

The husband is the protector as a rule, but she takes his part in the arguments at the inter-horde meetings. The women would urge the men to fight on such occasions; they delighted in the excitement and carried on their own private disputes on the sidelines so to speak. If a husband looked as though he were getting the worst of it, the wife might rush in regardless of her own danger, and either wrest the spears and boomerangs from him or else bodily drag him, reluctant and still struggling, off the field of battle.[1]

[1] Kaberry 1939, p. 141.

A further example is taken from Trotsky's *History of the Russian Revolution*.[1] Here the point seems to be that the women were relatively unlikely to be attacked, and for this reason were able to test out the soldiers' response to the revolutionaries' appeal for support:

. . . A great rôle is played by women workers in the relation between workers and soldiers. They go up to the cordons more boldly than men, take hold of the rifles, beseech, almost command: Put down your bayonets—join us. The soldiers are excited, ashamed, exchange anxious glances, waver; someone makes up his mind first, and the bayonets rise guiltily above the shoulders of the advancing crowd. The barrier is opened; a joyous and grateful Hurrah! shakes the air.

Finally, I shall cite Green's *Ibo village affairs*.[2] This author supports in a general way '. . . the recurrent notion that the women are to some extent the watchdogs of the community, the people who try to restore equilibrium when anti-social behaviour is on the increase.'[3] More specifically she discusses the importance of village exogamy in mitigating inter-village strife. Here the rôle of the women is structural in a more familiar way. The network of their links with their native villages affords a way for everybody to secure some measure of protection, in a situation which would otherwise be quite impossible:

The system of exogamy must have been one of the things that made inter-village or inter-village group trading a practical possibility. I have asked women how in the old days they would dare to go to the market of a village-group other than the one in which they were married and living. They have said that they would get one of the wives of their husbands' village-group, who had been born in the place holding the market and was therefore safe in it, to take them under her wing and accompany them.

. . . Powerful individuals could act as protectors to people travelling to market. But here again it would sometimes be through relatives-in-law that an introduction to such an individual could be gained.[4]

It seems to me that apart from the element of social control (to which I can think of no exact counterpart in animal societies) what is common to the above examples is that in relation to these situations of actual or potential conflict between men, the position of

---

[1] Trotsky, *The History of the Russian Revolution*, trans. Max Eastman 1936: I, 109. Cited by Goffman 1963, pp. 96–7 (footnote).

[2] Green 1947.   [3] ibid., p. 101.   [4] ibid.

the women is, for a number of reasons, a loosely defined one. This feature is at a structural level comparable to the 'equivocal' placing of the female in the dominance-based primate societies which I discussed above. It seems there often is something peculiar about the nature of females' (including women's) involvement in the map-making enactments of social life. This is not affected by the fact that in human societies this situation may arise through elements of social structure that are specifically human and cultural—such as patriliny and virilocal marriage.

It has not been possible in the course of this chapter to confine attention to the apparently simple issue of the position of females in relation to 'rank-orders' in animal and human groups. There is first of all the methodological problem created by treating the status hierarchy as coming first in the system. I have argued in addition that it is questionable, in all but the most obvious cases, to take animal and human hierarchical organizations as examples of the same thing until we have a more satisfactory 'minimal' definition of rank and the concepts connected with it. Related to this is the question, raised by at least one ethologist, whether we should be satisfied with the concept of 'dominance' even in ethological contexts. I do not think that this ultimately matters. The concept of 'dominance', looked at in one way, breaks down into systems whereby individuals acquire and possess differential 'rights' and 'obligations' in respect of resources such as food or space. (This applies equally to territorial systems.) One peculiarity about females may be that as well as being potential possessors they are also potential objects of these 'rights'. What may ultimately come of this line of enquiry is some minimal definition, appropriate to both human and animal situations, not only of 'rank' but of 'rights' as well. I suggest in addition that certain loosenesses in the position of females (notably among the human and non-human primates) could represent one group of possibilities for resolving a problem primitively 'given' in the nature of systems based on 'conspicuous participation' among males.

IX

CONCLUSIONS AND APPRAISALS

D ESPITE the chapter heading, it is not possible in a work of this scope to reach a conclusion in any but the temporal sense. I have experimented with what seemed initially to be four discrete topics, each of which looked like a promising area of contact between ethology and social anthropology. It turns out that they are not independent of one another at all, either in their specific subject matter or in the general—and, I think, important— issues to which they call attention. As far as the subject matter is concerned, Chapter V links up with Chapter VII via the ideas of 'effective face-to-face contact' and 'situational presence'. Chapter VI links up with Chapter VIII through the possibilities of women, by reason of their structural position in a society such as the Ibo, acting as instruments in the social control of warfare. It will be seen that at this level of comparison intra-tribal warfare becomes the equivalent of much animal aggressiveness, since both are amenable to control through being tied to a social organization. There are other connections between the subjects of the last four chapters, which are not worth spelling out. I shall conclude by trying to formulate some of the more general possibilities which this enquiry has begun to uncover, and to state, more explicitly than I have yet managed to do, the direction which I think the ethology/anthropology interdisciplinary effort must now take.

The four 'levels' of possible contact between ethology and social anthropology, which I discussed in Chapter IV, are now seen to be fairly artificial. It would have been quite impossible to keep them separate in any of the four chapters dealing with specific topics. But it is worth making use of them once more as a rough framework here.

I said in Chapter IV all that I had to say about the 'procedural' and 'pragmatic' aspects of the relationship between ethology and social anthropology. As far as the 'level' of data is concerned, I explored in Chapter V the failure of one attempt to link the social life of animals and men on the basis of a functional continuity between events occurring in both fields. I have emphasized several times that I do not wish to rule out functional comparisons between aspects of animal and human organization. My point is that the functional approach has been overplayed because it has been treated as the only possible approach. Lorenz for example treats it as such, at least in his discussions of the relationship between 'phyletic' and 'cultural' ritualization.[1] What does seem important at this 'level' of data is an idea I touched on in Chapter VI in connection with aggression (p. 93), that processes which contribute to social organization in animals may do the same for human society in a crude way, but more interestingly, in human society they are used and manipulated again and again, and form the basis for far-reaching social metaphors.[2] This is possibly part of what Freeman means by 'basic and pervasive processes which determine events at interrelated levels of behavioural integration.'[3]

Several times in the course of this book, and particularly in Chapters VII and VIII, I have been forced to ask questions about whether (roughly) 'the same sort of thing' is happening in human and animal cases. The attempt to distinguish these from questions which could be simply answered at the level of data (is man a territorial animal?) represents the beginning of a structural approach to ethological comparisons in human sociology. This attempt to develop a structural approach takes us, of course, on to a level of theory, but it also follows from procedural questions; what do we do to avoid the 'aha!-reaction' and the danger of question-begging classifications? The answer is that we probably cannot get round this difficulty entirely, but that we stand the best chance by returning to a kind of deductive start—by analysing the logical possibilities of social systems in different kinds of animals, and discovering what alternatives and combinations are open to them. We would hope to end up with a set of minimally defined, possibly interlinked, concepts which would form the simplest structural units in the analysis of all social organizations. We would then be in a position to see more clearly than at present what is specifically human about human societies. From this point we

---

[1] See Lorenz 1966a.
[2] Cf. Francis Huxley's view (1966) that certain Voodoo enactments represent a meeting of individual and social forces, whereby psycho-physiological events are utilized both to symbolize and to bring about a resolution of the mind–body problem.
[3] Freeman 1966.

could go on to enquire which of the differences between human societies represent real cleavages, and which represent variations on common structural themes. Such a procedure would necessitate an explicitly 'sociological' approach to social phenomena in animals; this move would not be unprecedented but might not be acceptable to all ethologists. Incidentally, such a move might offer to ethologists a partial escape route from the old instinct/learning problem, for it makes no sense to say of relationships and social facts that they are either 'innate' or 'learned'. Of course, once we have discovered the structural parameters of societies in this way we can presumably make higher-order functional statements involving them. For example I came near in Chapter VII to saying that meeting ceremonies 'function' as instruments of social classification—although I do not wish to claim that any fundamental 'structural parameter' has been uncovered in this case.

For social anthropology, the consequence of admitting the relevance of ethological comparisons in the way I have outlined might be neither more nor less than a redefinition of the social fact. This would come about not only in Freeman's sense[1] but also as a consequence of redefining the scope of sociological enquiry. I have hinted more than once that there might usefully be developed a sense of the term 'sociology' which would allow for sociological accounts (without quotation marks) of social phenomena in some non-human animals. I also suggested (p. 22) that a sociological level of analysis is implicit in many of the basic concepts of ethologists, and might as well be recognized and formulated by them.[2] Thus on the view I am putting forward, biological and sociological analysis would no longer belong to separate fields of discourse but would be seen to overlap and complement one another in the study of both human and animal social life. Social facts, on this view, are still those facts which are properly explored within a sociological framework—but this is no longer the exclusive definition it is commonly taken to be. We can now admit the relevance of both animal studies and statements about the 'biological heritage of man' to the investigation of social facts in human societies, without being guilty of any kind of biological reduction-

---

[1] ibid; and see Chapter 3 above (pp. 28–9).

[2] One obstacle to the achievement of this is the term 'behaviour' (especially 'social behaviour'), which covers a multitude of confusions. I have gone to some trouble to avoid this word whenever possible in this book.

ism. I submit that this adds enormous interest to the concept of the 'social fact.' Incidentally, the point I made in Chapter VI about the close relation between 'social control' and 'social structure' in both animals and man, can be held up against Durkheim's other definition of the social fact, that 'a social fact is to be recognized by the power of external coercion which it exercises or is capable of exercising over individuals.'[1]

It has been suggested to me that the relation between ethology and social anthropology parallels that holding between ecology and social anthropology; i.e. that we have to know how much of human social activity can be accounted for on 'biological' principles before we can begin to ask 'sociological' questions. I would agree, but with the proviso that no necessary opposition is involved between 'exclusively biological' and 'specifically sociological' thinking. What we need to know is how much of our social life is a product of the broadest principles of social organization as we can recognize it; then we can begin to see how much is contributed by our specifically human qualities, anatomical, physiological, genetic and social, and in what ways. The point was made to me by E. W. Ardener in connection with Chapter VIII that the existence of women in any society 'makes the meta-analytic function possible'; i.e. that the presence of at least two life-cycles and social patterns allows attention to be focused on the cycles and patterns themselves. Something very similar is central to the ethology/social anthropology programme. By spreading the net as widely as possible and taking note of every type and hint and rudiment of social organization that we can lay hands on, we stand the best possible chance of understanding what things are involved in 'social organization' itself.

[1] Durkheim 1895, p. 10.

X

POSTSCRIPT ON ETHOLOGISM

Whenever a new science achieves its first big successes, its enthusiastic acolytes always fancy that all question are now soluble by extension of its methods of solving its questions.[1]

ETHOLOGY is currently very fashionable indeed. One can hardly open a 'quality' Sunday newspaper without realizing that ethological jargon-words are now becoming popular catch-phrases. What used to be ethological in-jokes ('intellectual self-grooming') are now taken up by journalists with great solemnity and look like going the way of all technical terms which turn into popular clichés. Ethologists are naturally flattered by all this public attention. Because of their constant passing references to human affairs many are now in the position of one who says 'I've been telling you so for years'. Tinbergen[2] has recently tried to introduce some critical sobriety into the current enthusiasm for ethology. I would like to coin the term 'ethologism' as a label for the present vogue, shared by some ethologists with their popular/ educated audience, for invoking the findings of ethology as a necessary and sufficient explanation for large slices of human social life. In particular, I have in mind three recently published books and the public response they have stimulated: Lorenz's *On Aggression* (1966), Ardrey's *The Territorial Imperative* (1966) and Morris' *The Naked Ape* (1967).

There would be no point in attempting a detailed and critical account of these books. Each has been abundantly reviewed. In the course of this book I have had occasion to make certain specific criticisms of all three. It should be made clear perhaps that *The Territorial Imperative* does not belong in quite the same category as the other two works; its author is a journalist rather than a scientist, and (presumably) his motives consequently differ a little from those of Lorenz or Morris. But Ardrey's work is unquestionably a part of 'ethologism' as I have defined it.

[1] Ryle 1949, *The Concept of Mind*, p. 76.
[2] Tinbergen 1968.

POSTSCRIPT ON ETHOLOGISM   155

Many things irritate in *The Territorial Imperative*. It is easy to
grind one's teeth at Ardrey's jaunty journalistic style, his head-
patting manner towards distinguished authors ('Austria's Konrad
Lorenz and Holland's Niko Tinbergen'[1]), and his constant con-
spiratorial nudges at the reader. More serious is his superficial
treatment of evidence, as where he writes of Wynne-Edwards as
having 'demonstrated' that population homeostasis through territorial behaviour 'works'.[2] I have shown in Chapter v that Wynne-
Edwards has *demonstrated* nothing of the kind. Some would justify
papering over the doubts and qualifications of specialists in a
'popular' work, but I do not see why the 'general reader' should be
given the impression that scientific conclusions are simpler and
more unanimous than they are. In another instance, cited in
Chapter VIII (p. 136), Ardrey's distortion of the evidence on patas
monkeys amounts to a serious misrepresentation of his sources.[3]

When it comes to logic and argument the reader, happily, has
more of a chance. It requires no specialist knowledge to recognize
the following as an argument of the form 'if p then q; therefore, if
q then p':

I believe that our century has presented us with a means to demonstrate
that our attachment for property is of an ancient biological order. . . . I
suggested that the mysterious enhancement of powers which a territory
invariably summons in its male proprietor places energy otherwise un-
available at family disposal. If such enhancement of energy occurs in
man, then one cannot explain it as a cultural lesson.[4]

---

[1] p. 21.   [2] pp. 55–6.

[3] Cf. Ardrey on howler monkeys (p. 213) citing Carpenter's work on the
Barro Colorado group:
  '. . . Carpenter's careful observations showed that the mechanism isolating and
  integrating the howler clan is its defence of a social territory . . . The territories of howler clans are large, the borders vague . . .'
Here is what Carpenter actually says (the source is admittedly not one of
those cited by Ardrey):
  'It is a distortion of facts to draw boundary lines around howler ranges,
  because such lines convey the impression that the limits of ranges are sharp
  and distinct, closed rather than open, constant rather than fluid and variable.
  Howlers do not defend *boundaries* or whole territories; *they defend the place
  where they are*, and since they are most frequently in the familiar parts of their
  total ranges, these areas are most frequently defended . . . It can be seen that
  the "territory" concept holding that an animal or bird, or a group of them
  defends an exclusive space, den or nest does not describe accurately the behaviour of howler groups.' (1965, p. 273. Author's emphasis.)
[4] p. 103.

This is not an isolated instance of logical sharp practice on Ardrey's part. Another example may be found on pp. 136-7, where in quick succession he explains the homing of salmon, and their territoriality in an immature phase, in terms of one another. What he seems to mean is that the homing provides the functional explanation of the territoriality, and that the territoriality, in some sense, furnishes a mechanical explanation of the homing. But it is not at all clear how these relationships might hold; it seems to have been easier for Ardrey to obscure the differences between these types of explanation with a great deal of rhetorical writing about the still unsolved problem of how the fish actually find their way. This lack of scruple must exclude Ardrey's book from serious consideration as a work of scholarship. I think this is a pity on the whole, for some of his ideas (such as the difference between societies held together by inward and by outward antagonisms) could well be pursued by ethologists and sociologists on an interdisciplinary basis.

Morris, because of his avowedly ethnocentric point of view in *The Naked Ape*, risks being dismissed from the start by anybody interested in comparative sociology. He writes for example:

To begin with we must establish precisely how the naked ape does behave today when indulging in sexual behaviour. This is not as easy as it sounds, because of the great variability that exists, both between and within societies. The only solution is to take average results from large samples of the most successful societies. The small, backward and unsuccessful societies can largely be ignored. They may have fascinating and bizarre sexual customs, but biologically speaking they no longer represent the mainstream of evolution. Indeed it may very well be that their unusual sexual behaviour has helped to turn them into biological failures as social groups.[1]

It is enormously difficult, even in conversation, to reconcile the zoologist's and sociologist's points of view on the kinds of question that can be asked about societies. This is principally because so many zoologists, like Morris, do not recognize that there is any problem. They themselves have a comparatively easy life as far as theory goes; and they tend to assume that once you have found out about a society's adaptation to its environment, and perhaps uncovered a 'survival value' for a few of its institutions, you have

[1] pp. 50-1.

fully described the situation. Now one can indeed ask these questions about societies in a very broad way; they are important, perhaps, chiefly because it is only when they have been answered that sociological enquiry can begin. But to take up an attitude such as Morris reveals is to be, quite simply, unscientific. There are real differences between 'primitive' and 'modern' societies, as Mary Douglas has convincingly shown.[1] But who says that our particular European culture is the *only* successful one, and therefore has exclusive rights to represent 'the mainstream' of human evolution? Agreed, we are economically and technologically successful, but Morris is talking about biological success in some unspecified sense. It might have helped if he had distinguished between the 'success' of social systems and that of populations. But even if he had given us a clear criterion for evaluating the 'success' of either, it would not follow that *every* characteristic of the successful culture or group carried a biological blessing. Morris' discussion of 'pair-bonding' in the human species, for example, comes to look pretty silly when we realize that it rests on the assumption that because Western society is on the whole monogamous, monogamy is the only 'successful' pattern of human marriage (or does he mean mating?). Even on his own assumptions, Morris is on shaky ground, for Lorenz himself has remarked that 'in the evolutionary process you find everything that is just good enough for survival.'

In fact, Morris uses evidence only from British/American culture, and this makes one suspect that his real reason for restricting the field in this way is a lack (or perhaps a superabundance!) of comparative ethnographic material of a systematic kind. One would not be so far out of sympathy with him if he had honestly said so.

Apart from exposing this one glaring mistake, I feel that it would be missing the point of *The Naked Ape* to try to evaluate it on zoological grounds or to go too closely into the logic of some of Morris' speculations. Both Morris' and Ardrey's books have an undeniable appeal; they are entertainingly and sometimes spectacularly written. Lorenz is rapidly acquiring the charisma of a 'sage of our times'. (I note from *The Times* of 29th June 1968 that it is now possible for people to be called 'followers of Konrad Lorenz'.[2]) The real significance of these three very different books is to be

---

[1] Douglas 1966.
[2] Review by Edward Candy of Antony Storr's *Human Aggression*.

understood only by looking at this general phenomenon of 'ethologism' which is currently upon us.[1]

Intrinsic to ethologism is the conviction that now is the time when our thinking about ourselves must be pushed in a new direction. Thus Lorenz places himself in the category of middle-range innovators who 'can flatter (themselves) that (they) have something to say that is "due" to be said at that moment.'[2] In Chapter III I mentioned the current concern among some social anthropologists about an urgent need to revise certain assumptions of social science and to bring them into line with biological thinking. Obviously the two phenomena are not independent of each other, although the one is taking place in a 'popular', the other in a specialist, context. I feel that the 'now' aspect of ethologism can be partly understood if we realize that ethologism is the current attempt to answer some very old questions—questions about where humanity fits into the universe, whether 'the universe' refers to the world of matter or the world of life. Lorenz himself makes this quite clear:

Expert teaching of biology is the one and only foundation on which really sound opinion about mankind and its relation to the universe can be built. Philosophical anthropology of a type neglecting biological fact has done its worst by imbuing humanity with that sort of pride which not only comes before, but causes a fall. It is plain biology of *Homo sapiens L.* that ought to be considered the 'big science'.[3]

Ethologism, I submit, is the outcome of the following combination. A general desire to uncover the fundamental realities of human nature has been a constant feature of European thought, certainly since the Age of Enlightenment. This, in its current form, happens to coincide at the moment with a widespread and well-founded gloom about the human condition and our prospects for survival as a species. In addition we must take into account the changing ways in which 'animal instincts' have fitted into the picture of human life.

It is well known that the 'evolutionary mentality' of the nine-

---

[1] While this work was under revision, there appeared a collection of essays most of which treat Lorenz and Ardrey as one man and attack their books from the standpoint that 'the notion [of the existence of instincts in man] has no scientific validity whatever.' (M. F. Ashley Montague (ed.), *Man and Aggression*; Oxford University Press paperback, 1968.) This obviously heralds a movement which I am delighted to label 'anti-ethologism'.

[2] Lorenz 1966, p. 237.   [3] ibid., p. 257.

teenth century demanded to know the origins of everything, including social forms and institutions (see Chapter II). This is not too far from the 'romantic' longing to discover the 'roots of our being', whether as individuals or as a society. Such a desire, it seems likely, motivated a good deal of early anthropology from the Noble Savage on, and possibly persists as an undercurrent in intellectual life even now. It may have something to do with the more modern anthropological idea that through studying the 'simpler' organization of 'preliterate' peoples we can work towards an understanding of the basic elements of our own social life. But 'the savage' for this purpose has long been played out, partly because of the discrediting of older evolutionary ideas, but also (and more importantly for 'romanticism' on a popular front) because he has gradually ceased to fulfil yet another requirement of 'romantic' thought—the requirement that the thing one seeks to understand should be remote, the understanding of it comfortably unattainable. Added to this is a strong disillusionment with the whole of the human condition, not just the 'civilized' condition. Freeman for example holds a pessimistic view of humanity in its 'natural' state which goes straight back to Hobbes:

With . . . few exceptions, the ethnographic evidence shows warfare among primitive peoples to have been endemic, and, on occasion, internecine. Among some of the most primitive populations, indeed, aggressive behaviour is so endemic between groups as to dominate all aspects of their existence. Such a people are the Willigiman-Wallalua, of the Baliem valley of Western New Guinea, whose lives are 'an unending round of death and revenge' . . . Here I would suggest we have revealed the essentials of the pristine state of man.[1]

The influence of psychoanalysis, too, must not be forgotten.

Ethologism neatly resolves all these difficulties at one stroke, by replacing the savage by the animal. We can no longer happily locate the roots of our nature in primal man or in primitive society —but we can locate them in the animal quietly going about its business. We can even discern there the innocence which we feel ought to belong to our origins but which we can no longer quite believe in as a human virtue. Ethology seems to furnish us with an impeccable licence to revitalize our values by redefining them in biological terms. Consider Lorenz's comfortingly simple

[1] Freeman 1964.

biological definition of evil,[1] and Morris' notion of 'biological morality'.[2] Ethologism is even able to furnish the 'unattainability' clause; Lorenz at least is dead on target when he assures us that 'the scientist knows very well that he is approaching ultimate truth only in an asymptotic curve and is barred from ever reaching it.'[3] On the other hand ethologism in general is more accurately described by Ryle's remark which I quoted at the head of this chapter.

Ethologism finally clicks into place when we look at the ways in which the instincts and behaviour of animals have fitted into European intellectuals' attempts to understand themselves. I have gone over much of this ground in Chapter II. The 'mental evolution' writers, as we saw, placed the mental life of animals on a continuum with our own; and Darwin was keenly concerned to show that the rudiments of morality and social responsibility were found in the behaviour of the higher animals. At roughly the same time, 'Social Darwinism' took up the other theme of ruthless competitiveness in the animal world. Both schools were discredited, and replaced by the behaviourists' return to a strictly dualistic position in the Cartesian tradition. This rapidly became part of a broad consensus of *tabula rasa* thinking, which is only now beginning to give way in places. (Chomsky's view of the species-specific basis of language seems to constitute one of these cracks.) Now, the wheel is turning full circle. For better or worse, animal behaviour is 'back'. The improved concepts and techniques of ethology are revealing hitherto unsuspected degrees of subtlety and sophistication in the behaviour and social organization of animals. Some of this material has been discussed in the course of this inquiry. This comes across at the popular level as the discovery that 'animals can solve their problems much better than we can.' Hence ethologism. Ethologism, then, is compounded of something like romanticism, plus the current gloom and despondency about the human condition, plus the perfectly genuine successes of ethology as a science.

Ethologism gains much of its character from a peculiar combination of attraction and resistance in the public mind towards biologically oriented explanations of our behaviour. The attractions we already know something about. The resistances go back a long way, for they are surely continuous with the earlier, ideological

---

[1] Lorenz 1966, p. 134ff.   [2] Morris 1967, pp. 98–102.
[3] Lorenz 1966, p. 248.

barriers between animal and human mental life. This public reluctance has been recognized and played up to in all three of the books I have been considering, as where Morris points out that we, like all *nouveaux riches*, are 'sensitive about our background'.[1] Lorenz as usual goes most thoughtfully into the question in his chapter 'On the virtue of scientific humility.'[2] The situation has been accurately summed up, I think, by Horton: '. . . one would expect the "pollution anxieties" attendant on trying to cross the human/non-human barrier to be far more intense than those that marked the crossing from the non-living to the living . . .'[3] These resistances are linked, paradoxically, with another factor which works on the side of ethologism: the public taste for castigation from experts. Biologists and ethologists are the current experts, as were the stern clerics of an earlier age whose sermons seem to have whipped up so much public indulgence.

Ethologism, I should like to suggest, offers an origin myth of a novel kind—an original and powerful variation on the Garden of Eden theme. To some indeed it offers a charter myth:

. . . we are now released—those of us who have felt guilty every time we enjoyed our own property, bewildered at all the men who adore the trappings of war, miserable because every decently rehoused set of underdogs instantly tries to become top dog of the kennel, uncomprehending of the amount of sheer pleasure one seems to get from battling with one's enemies.

. . . The desire to have and to hold, to screech at the neighbours and say 'Mine, all mine' is in our nature too. Ardrey and his allies have let us off perfection and I for one feel a lot better for it.'[4]

In addition, ethologism is in some respects very like a cargo cult. We are asked to sacrifice certain prejudices and beliefs about our unique and privileged position in the evolutionary world. In return we are promised two kinds of control; cognitive control of a bewildering state of affairs and practical control of a dangerous one. 'Sufficient knowledge of man and of his position in the universe would . . . automatically determine the ideals for which we have to strive.'[5] This element of practical and urgently needed control completes the explanation of the 'now' component of ethologism.

[1] Morris 1967, p.241.   [2] Lorenz 1966, pp. 189–203.
[3] Horton 1961.   [4] Katherine Whitehorn, *The Observer*, 29 October 1967.
[5] Lorenz 1966, p. 257.

BIBLIOGRAPHY

AINSWORTH, MARY D., 1963: 'The Development of Infant–mother Interaction among the Ganda', in Foss (ed.), *Determinants of Infant Behaviour* (London, Methuen), Vol. II, 67–104.

ALTMANN, S. A., 1962: 'Social behaviour of anthropoid primates: analysis of recent concepts', in Bliss (ed.), *Roots of Behaviour* (New York, Harper), 277–85.

ANDRESKI, STANISLAV, 1964: 'Origins of war', in Carthy and Ebling (eds.), *The Natural History of Aggression*, 129–36.

ANDREW, R. J., 1963: 'The origin and evolution of the calls and facial expressions of the primates', *Behaviour*, 20, 1–109.

ARDENER, E. W., 1965: review of Jarvie's *The Revolution in Social Anthropology*, in *Man*, LXV, 57.

ARDENER, E. W., 1967: answer to A. S. A. request for comment on *The Modern Rôle of Social Anthropology* (mimeo).

ARDREY, ROBERT, 1966: *The Territorial Imperative* (London, Collins, 1967).

ARGYLE, MICHAEL, 1967: *The Psychology of Interpersonal Behaviour* (Penguin Books).

BARNETT, S. A. (ed.), 1962: *Lessons from Animal Behaviour for the Clinician* (London, Little Club Clinics in Developmental Medicine, No. 7).

BARNETT, S. A. and EVANS, C. S., 1965: 'Questions on the social dynamics of rodents', in Ellis, P. E. (ed.), *Social Organization of Animal Communities* (*Symposia of the Zoological Society of London*, No. 14).

BEATTIE, J., 1964: definition of 'Ethnography' in Gould and Kolb (eds.), *Dictionary of the Social Sciences*, 245–6.

BENEDICT, R., 1934: *Patterns of Culture* (Mentor Books edn., 1948).

BERNE, ERIC, 1966: *Games People Play* (London, Deutsch).

BIERENS DE HAAN, J. A., 1948: 'Animal psychology and the science of animal behaviour', *Behaviour*, 1, 71–80.

Blest, A. D., 1961: 'The concept of "ritualization"', in Thorpe and Zangwill (eds.), *Current Problems in Animal Behaviour* (Cambridge, C.U.P.), 102–24.

BLURTON JONES, N. G., 1967: 'An ethological study of some aspects of social behaviour of children in nursery school', in Morris (ed.), *Primate Ethology* (London, Weidenfeld & Nicolson), 347–68.

BOYD, HUGH, 1953: 'On encounters between wild white-fronted geese in winter flocks', *Behaviour*, 5, 85–129.

BRIAN, ANNE D., 1949: 'Dominance in the great tit, *Parus major*', *Scottish Naturalist*, 61, 144–55.

BROWN, J. L. and HUNSPERGER, R. W., 1963: 'Neuroethology and the motivation of agonistic behaviour', *Animal Behaviour*, 11, 439–48.

BROWN, ROBERT, 1963: *Explanation in Social Science* (London, Routledge and Kegan Paul).

BRUNER, E. M., 1964: 'The psychological approach in anthropology', in Tax (ed.), *Horizons of Anthropology* (London, Allen and Unwin), 71–80.

BURROW, J. W., 1966: *Evolution and Society: A Study in Victorian Social Theory* (Cambridge, C.U.P.).

BURTON, JOHN, 1964: 'The nature of aggression as revealed in the atomic age', in Carthy and Ebling (eds.), *The Natural History of Aggression*, 145–53.

CALHOUN, J. B., 1962: 'A behavioural sink', in Bliss (ed.), *Roots of Behaviour* (New York, Harper), 295–315.

CALHOUN, J. B., 1966: 'The rôle of space in animal sociology', *Journal of Social Issues*, XXII, 4, 46–58.

CARPENTER, C. R., 1942: 'Sexual behaviour of free ranging rhesus monkeys (*Macaca mulatta*)', *Journal of Comparative Psychology*, 33, 113–62.

CARPENTER, C. R., 1958: 'Territoriality: A review of concepts and problems', in Roe and Simpson (eds.), *Behaviour and Evolution* (Newhaven, Yale University Press), 224–50.

CARPENTER, C. R., 1965: 'The howlers of Barro Colorado Island', in De Vore (ed.), *Primate Behaviour* (New York, Holt, Rinehart and Winston), 250–91.

CARR-SAUNDERS, A., 1922: *The Population Problem* (Oxford, Clarendon Press).

CARTHY, J. D. and EBLING, F. J. (eds.), 1964: *The Natural History of Aggression*, I. B. Symposia, No. 13 (London, Academic Press).

CHANCE, M. R. A., 1962: 'An interpretation of some agonistic postures: the role of "cut-off" acts and postures' (*Symposia of the Zoological Society of London*, No. 8), 71–89.

CHANCE, M. R. A., 1963: 'The social bond of the primates', *Primates*, 4, 4.

CHANCE, M. R. A., 1967: 'Attention structure as the basis of primate rank orders', *Man*, NS 2, 4.

CONDER, P. J., 1949: 'Individual distance', *Ibis*, 91, 649–55.

CROOK, J. H., 1961: 'The basis of flock organization in birds', in Thorpe and Zangwill (eds.), *Current Problems in Animal Behaviour* (Cambridge, C.U.P.), 125–49.

CROOK, J. H., 1965: 'The adaptive significance of avian social organizations', in Ellis (ed.), *Social Organization of Animal Communities*

(*Symposia of the Zoological Society of London*, No. 14), 181–218.

CROOK, J. H., 1967: comment on Reynolds, 1966, in *Man*, NS 2, 1, 131.

DARWIN, CHARLES, 1871: *The Descent of Man* (2nd edn. 1899).

DARWIN, F. (ed.), 1887: *Life and Letters of Charles Darwin*.

DAVENPORT, W., 1963: 'Social Organization', in Siegel (ed.), *Biennial Review of Anthropology*, 178–228.

DAVIS, D. E., 1962: 'An enquiry into the Phylogeny of Gangs', in Bliss (ed.), *Roots of Behaviour* (New York, Harper), 316–20.

DAVIS, D. E., 1964: 'The Physiological analysis of aggressive behaviour', in Etkin (ed.), *Social Behaviour and Organization among Vertebrates* (Chicago and London, University of Chicago Press), 53–72.

DEVONS, E. and GLUCKMAN, M., 1964: 'Modes and consequences of limiting a field of study', concluding chapter to Gluckman (ed.), *Closed Systems and Open Minds* (Edinburgh, Oliver & Boyd).

DOUGLAS, MARY, 1966: *Purity and Danger* (London, Routledge and Kegan Paul).

DOUGLAS, MARY, 1966a: 'Population control in primitive groups', *British Journal of Sociology*, 1966, 263.

DURBIN, E. F. M. and BOWLBY, J., 1939: 'Personal Aggressiveness and War', in Durbin and Catlin (eds.), *War and Democracy: Essays on the Causes and Prevention of War* (London, Kegan Paul).

DURKHEIM, E., 1895: *Rules of Sociological Method* (Free Press Paperback, 1938).

ELWIN, VERRIER, 1943: *Maria Murder and Suicide* (London, O.U.P.).

ETKIN, W., 1964: 'Co-operation and competition in social behaviour', in Etkin (ed.), *Social Behaviour and Organization among Vertebrates* (Chicago and London, University of Chicago Press), 1–34.

ETKIN, W., 1964a: 'Types of social organization in birds and mammals', in Etkin, (ed.), *Social Behaviour and Organization among Vertebrates* (Chicago and London, University of Chicago Press), 256–95.

EVANS-PRITCHARD, E. E., 1940: *The Nuer* (Oxford, Clarendon Press).

EVANS-PRITCHARD, E. E., 1950: 'Social anthropology, past and present' (the Marett Lecture), republished 1962 in *Essays in Social Anthropology* (London, Faber and Faber), 13–28.

EVANS-PRITCHARD, E. E., 1955: 'The position of women in primitive societies and in our own', republished 1965 in *The Position of Women and Other Essays*, (London, Faber and Faber).

EVANS-PRITCHARD, E. E., 1963: 'The comparative method in social anthropology', reprinted in *The Position of Women* (1965).

FIRTH, R., 1951: 'Contemporary British social anthropology', *American Anthropologist*, 53, 474–89.

FLETCHER, RONALD, 1957: *Instinct in Man* (New York, International Universities Press).

Fox, Robin, 1967: 'In the beginning: Aspects of Hominid behavioural evolution' (the Malinowski Lecture), *Man*, NS 2, 3, 415–33.

Fox, Robin, 1967a: *Kinship and Marriage* (Pelican Books).

Freeman, Derek, 1964: 'Human aggression in anthropological perspective', in Carthy and Ebling (eds.), *The Natural History of Aggression*, 109–19.

Freeman, Derek, 1965: 'Anthropology, psychiatry and the doctrine of cultural relativism', *Man*, LXV, 65–7.

Freeman, Derek, 1966: 'Social anthropology and the scientific study of human behaviour', *Man*, NS 1, 330–42.

Geertz, C., 1964: 'The Transition to Humanity', in Tax (ed.), *Horizons of Anthropology* (London, Allen and Unwin), 37–49.

Ginsberg, Morris, 1961: *Evolution and Progress*, Vol. 3 of Essays in Sociology and Social Philosophy (London, Heinemann).

Gluckman, M., 1944: 'The difficulties, achievements and limitations of social anthropology', reprinted from *Rhodes–Livingstone Journal*, 1.

Gluckman, M. (ed.), 1964: *Closed Systems and Open Minds: The Limits of Naïveté in Social Anthropology* (Edinburgh, Oliver and Boyd).

Goffman, Erving, 1963: *Behaviour in Public Places* (New York, Free Press of Glencoe).

Goodall, Jane, 1965: 'Chimpanzees of the Gombe Stream Reserve', in De Vore (ed.), *Primate Behaviour* (New York, Holt, Rinehart and Winston), 425–73.

Grant, Ewan C., 1965: 'An ethological description of some schizophrenic patterns of behaviour', reprinted from *Proceedings of the Leeds Symposium of Behavioural Disorders.*

Grant, Ewan C. and Chance, M. R. A., 1958: 'Rank order in caged rats', *Animal Behaviour*, 6, 183–94

Gray, P. H., 1958: 'Theory and evidence of imprinting in human infants', *Journal of Psychology*, 46, 155.

Green, M.M., 1947: *Ibo Village Affairs* (London, Sidgwick and Jackson).

Hafez, E. S. E. *et al.*, 1962: 'The behaviour of horses', in Hafez (ed.), *Behaviour of Domestic Animals* (London, Baillière, Tindall and Cox), 370–96.

Hale, E. B., 1962: 'Domestication and the evolution of behaviour', in Hafez (ed.), *Behaviour of Domestic Animals*, 21–53.

Hall, Edward T., 1955: 'The anthropology of manners', *Scientific American*, April 1955, 84–90.

Hall, Edward T., 1963: 'A system for the notation of proxemic behaviour', *American Anthropologist*, 65, 1003–26.

Hall, K. R. L., 1962: 'The sexual, agonistic and derived social behaviour patterns of the wild Chacma Baboon, *Papio Ursinus*', *Proceedings of the Zoological Society of London*, 139, 283–327.

HALL, K. R. L., 1963: 'Ecology of the Chacma Baboon', *Symposia of the Zoological Society of London*, No. 10, 1–28.

HALL, K. R. L., 1964: 'Aggression in monkey and ape societies,' in Carthy and Ebling (eds.), *The Natural History of Aggression*, 51–64.

HALL, K. R. L. *et al.*, 1965: 'Behaviour of Patas monkeys, *Erythrocebus patas*, in captivity, with notes on the natural habitat', *Folia Primatologica*, 3, 22–49.

HALL, K. R. L. and DE VORE, IRVEN, 1965: 'Baboon social behaviour', in De Vore (ed.), *Primate Behaviour* (New York, Holt, Rinehart and Winston), 53–110.

HALSEY, A. H., 1967: 'Sociology, Biology and Population Control' (the Galton Lecture), typescript.

HAMPSHIRE, STUART, 1968: 'Conversation with Noam Chomsky on philosophy and linguistics', *The Listener*, Vol. 79, No. 2044 (30th May).

HARLOW, HARRY F., 1962: 'The heterosexual affectional system in monkeys', *American Psychologist*, 17, 1–9.

HARRISON MATTHEWS, L., 1964: 'Overt fighting in mammals', in Carthy and Ebling (eds.), *The Natural History of Aggression*, 23–32.

HEDIGER, H., 1955: *Studies of the Psychology and Behaviour of Captive Animals in Zoos and Circuses* (London, Butterworth's Scientific Publications).

HEDIGER, H., 1965: 'Man as a social partner of animals and vice versa', in Ellis (ed.), *Social Organization of Animal Communities* (*Symposia of the Zoological Society of London*, No. 14), 291–300.

HESS, ECKHARD H., 1962: 'Ethology: an approach towards the complete analysis of behaviour', in Brown *et al.*, *New Directions in Psychology* (New York, Holt, Rinehart and Winston), 157–266.

Hill, D., 1964: 'Aggression and mental illness', in Carthy and Ebling (eds.), *The Natural History of Aggression*, 91–9.

HINDE, R. A., 1959: 'Some recent trends in ethology', in Koch (ed.), *Psychology: A Study of a Science* (New York, McGraw-Hill), Vol. II, 561–610.

HINDE, R. A., 1961: 'The establishment of the parent–offspring relation in birds, with some mammalian analogies', in Thorpe and Zangwill, (eds.), *Current Problems in Animal Behaviour* (Cambridge, C.U.P.), 175–93.

HINDE, R. A., 1962: 'The relevance of animal studies to human neurotic disorders', in Richter *et al.* (eds.), *Aspects of Psychiatric Research* (London, O.U.P.), 240–61.

HINDE, R. A. and TINBERGEN, N., 1958: 'The comparative study of species-specific behaviour', in Roe and Simpson (eds.), *Behaviour and Evolution* (New Haven, Yale University Press), 251–68.

HIRSCH, LINDLEY and TOLMAN, 1955: 'An experimental test of an alleged innate sign stimulus', *Journal of Comparative and Physio-logical Psychology*, 48, 278–80.

HOCKETT, C. F. and ASCHER, R., 1964: 'The human revolution', *Current Anthropology*, 5, 135–47.

HOEBEL, E. ADAMSON, 1964: definition of 'ethnocentrism' in Gould and Kolb (eds.), *Dictionary of the Social Sciences*, 245.

HORTON, W. R. G., 1961: 'Social Science, logical or psychological impossibility?', *Man* LXI, 11

HUIZINGA, J., 1949: *Homo Ludens: A Study of the Play-Element in Culture* (London, International Library of Sociology and Social Reconstruction).

HUME, C. W., 1959: 'In praise of anthropomorphism,' *Animal Behaviour*, 7, 248–9.

HUXLEY, F. J., 1966: 'The ritual of Voodoo and the symbolism of the body', in Huxley (ed.), *Ritualization of Behaviour in Animals and Man*, (Philosophical Transactions of the Royal Society, London, Vol. 251, No. 772).

HUXLEY, J. S., 1914: 'The courtship of the Great Crested Grebe', *Proceedings of the Royal Society, London*, 11, 491–562.

HUXLEY, J. S., 1955: 'Evolution, cultural and biological', reprinted from *Yearbook of Anthropology*.

HUXLEY, J. S., 1958: 'Cultural process and evolution', in Roe and Simpson (eds.), *Behaviour and Evolution* (New Haven, Yale University Press), 437–54.

HUXLEY, J. S., 1962: 'Higher and Lower Organization in evolution', reprinted from *Journal of the Royal College of Surgeons of Edinburgh*, 7, 163–79.

HUXLEY, J. S. (ed.), 1966: *Ritualization of Behaviour in Animals and Man* (Philosophical Transactions of the Royal Society, London, Vol. 251, No. 772).

HUXLEY, T. H., 1887: 'On the reception of *The Origin of Species*', in Darwin, F. (ed.), *Life and Letters of Charles Darwin*, Vol. 2, 179–204.

IMANISHI, KINJI, 1960: 'Social organization of subhuman primates in their natural habitat', *Current Anthropology*, 1, 393–407.

JARVIE, I. C., 1964: *The Revolution in Social Anthropology* (London, International Library of Sociology and Social Reconstruction).

JAY, PHYLLIS, 1965: 'The common langur of North India', in De Vore (ed.), *Primate Behaviour* (New York, Holt, Rinehart and Winston), 197–249.

KABERRY, PHYLLIS, 1939: *Aboriginal Woman* (London, Routledge).

KALMUS, H., 1965: 'Origins and general features', in Ellis (ed.), *Social Organization of Animal Communities* (*Symposia of the Zoological Society of London*, No. 14), 1–12.

KATZ, DAVID, 1937: *Animals and Men: Studies in Comparative Psychology* (London, Longmans, Green and Co.).

KENNEDY, J. S., 1954: 'Is modern ethology objective?', *British Journal of Animal Behaviour*, 2, 12–19.

KLOPFER, P. H. and HAILMAN, J. P., 1967: *An introduction to Animal Behaviour: Ethology's First Century* (New Jersey, Prentice-Hall).

KORTLANDT, A. and KOOIJ, M., 1963: 'Protohominid behaviour in primates' (*Symposia of the Zoological Society of London*, No. 10.) 61–88.

KROEBER, A. L. and WATERMAN, T. T., 1931: *Source Book in Anthropology* (New York, Harcourt, Brace & Co.).

KUMMER, HANS, 1968; *Social Organisation of Hamadryas Baboons* (Basel, S. Karger).

KUMMER, H. and KURT, F., 1963: 'Social units of a free-living population of Hamadryas Baboons', *Folia Primatologica*, 1, 4–19.

LA FONTAINE, G., 1960: 'Homicide and suicide among the Gisu', in Bohannan (ed.), *African Homicide and Suicide* (Princeton University Press), 94–129.

LEACH, E. R., 1966: 'Ritualization in man in relation to conceptual and social development', in Huxley (ed.), *Ritualization of Behaviour in Animals and Man* 403–8.

LENNEBERG, E. H., 1964: 'A biological Perspective of Language', in Lenneberg, (ed.), *New Directions in the Study of Language* (Cambridge, Mass., M.I.T.), 65–89.

LEYHAUSEN, PAUL, 1965: 'Communal organization of solitary mammals', in Ellis (ed.), *Social Organization of Animal Communities* (*Symposia of the Zoological Society of London*, No. 14), 249–63.

LIENHARDT, R. G., 1963: 'On the concept of objectivity in social anthropology' (the second Malinowski Lecture), reprinted from *Journal of the Royal Anthropological Institute*, 94.

LIENHARDT, R. G., 1964: *Social Anthropology* (London, O.U.P.).

LORENZ, K. Z., 1935: 'Companionship in bird life', republished 1957 in Schiller (ed.), *Instinctive Behaviour* (New York, International Universities Press), 83-116.

LORENZ, K. Z., 1956: 'The objectivistic theory of instinct', in Grassé *et al.*, *L'instinct dans le comportement des animaux et de l'homme* (Paris, Masson), 51–64.

LORENZ, K. Z., 1964: 'Ritualized fighting', in Carthy and Ebling (eds.), *The Natural History of Aggression*, 39–50.

LORENZ, K. Z., 1965: *Evolution and Modification of Behaviour* (London, Methuen, 1966).

LORENZ, K. Z., 1966: *On Aggression* (London, Methuen).

LORENZ, K. Z., 1966a: 'Evolution of ritualization in the biological and cultural spheres', in Huxley (ed.), *Ritualization of Behaviour in Animals and Man*, 273–84.

LOWENSTEIN, O., 1964: 'Descartes, Mechanistic biology and animal behaviour', *Animal Behaviour*, Suppl. I, 109–11.

LOWIE, R. H., 1937: *The History of Ethnological Theory* (London, Harrap).

MALINOWSKI, B., 1926: *Crime and Custom in Savage Society* (London, International Library of Psychology, Philosophy and Scientific Method).

MALINOWSKI, B., 1939: Preface to Fei, Hsiao-Tung, *Peasant Life in China* (London, Routledge).

MARETT, R. R., 1936: *Tylor* (London, Chapman and Hall).

MEAD, MARGARET, 1949: *Male and Female* (London, Gollancz).

MORRIS, DESMOND, 1957: ' "Typical intensity" and its relation to the problem of ritualization', *Behaviour*, 11, 1–13.

MORRIS, DESMOND, 1967: *The Naked Ape* (London, Cape).

MURDOCK, G. P., 1951: 'British social anthropology', *American Anthropologist*, 53, 465–73.

MCBRIDE, ARTHUR and HEBB, D. O., 1948: 'Behaviour of the captive Bottlenose Dolphin, *Tursiops truncatus*', *Journal of Comparative Psychology*, 41, 111–23.

NADEL, S. F., 1951: *Foundations of Social Anthropology* (London, Cohen and West).

NADEL, S. F., 1956: 'Culture and Personality: A re-examination,' reprinted from *Medical Journal of Australia*, 8th Dec. 1956, 845.

REYNOLDS, V. and F., 1965: 'Chimpanzees of the Budongo Forest', in De Vore (ed.), *Primate Behaviour* (New York, Holt, Rinehart and Winston), 368–424.

REYNOLDS, V., 1966: 'Open groups in hominid evolution', *Man*, NS 1, 4, 441–52.

RIFKIN, A. M., 1963: 'Violence in human behaviour', *Science*, 140, 904–6.

ROWELL, T. E., 1967: 'Variability in the social organization of primates', in Morris (ed.), *Primate Ethology* (London, Weidenfeld & Nicolson), 219–35.

RUSSELL, CLAIRE and RUSSELL, W. M. S., 1968: *Violence, Monkeys and Man* (London, Macmillan)

RYLE, GILBERT, 1949: *The Concept of Mind* (London, Hutchinson).

SAHLINS, MARSHALL D., 1959: 'The social life of monkeys, apes and primitive man', in Spuhler (ed.), *The Evolution of Man's Capacity for Culture* (Detroit, Wayne State University Press), 54–73.

SAHLINS, MARSHALL D., 1960: 'The origin of Society', reprinted from *Scientific American*, Sept. 1960.

SAWER, GEOFFREY, 1965: *Law in Society* (Oxford, Clarendon Law Series).

SCHALLER, GEORGE B., 1965: 'The behaviour of the mountain gorilla', in De Vore (ed.), *Primate Behaviour* (New York, Holt, Rinehart and Winston), 324–67.

SCOTT, J. P., 1958: *Aggression* (Chicago, University of Chicago Press).

SCOTT, J. P., 1962: 'Hostility and aggression in animals', in Bliss (ed.), *Roots of Behaviour* (New York, Harper), 167.

SCOTT, J. P. and Fuller, J. L., 1965: *Genetics and the Social Behaviour of the Dog* (Chicago and London, University of Chicago Press).

SIMONDS, PAUL E., 1965: 'The Bonnet Macaque in South India', in De Vore (ed.), *Primate Behaviour* (New York, Holt, Rinehart and Winston), 175–96.

SIMPSON, G. G., 1958: 'The study of evolution', in Roe and Simpson (eds.), *Behaviour and Evolution* (New Haven, Yale University Press), 7–26.

SOMMER, ROBERT, 1959: 'Studies in personal space', *Sociometry*, 22, 247–60.

SOUTHALL. A. W., 1960: 'Homicide and suicide among the Alur', in Bohannan (ed.), *African Homicide and Suicide* (Princeton University Press), 214–29.

SPENCER, HERBERT, 1904: *Autobiography* (London, Williams and Norgate).

SPUHLER, J. N., 1959: 'Somatic paths to culture', in Spuhler (ed.), *Evolution of Man's Capacity for Culture* (Detroit, Wayne State University Press), 1–13.

STORR, ANTHONY, 1964: 'Possible substitutes for war', in Carthy and Ebling (eds.), *The Natural History of Aggression*, 137–44.

THOMPSON, W. R., 1958: 'Social Behaviour', in Roe and Simpson (eds.), *Behaviour and Evolution* (New Haven, Yale University Press), 291–310.

THURNWALD, HILDE, 1934: 'Woman's status in Buin society', *Oceania*, V, 141–170.

TIGER, LIONEL and FOX, ROBIN, 1966: 'The zoological perspective in social science', *Man*, NS 1, 75–81.

TINBERGEN, N., 1948: 'Social releasers and the experimental method required for their study', *Wilson Bulletin*, 60, 6–51 (cited in Hirsch, Lindley and Tolman, 1955).

TINBERGEN, N., 1951: *The Study of Instinct* (Oxford, Clarendon Press).

TINBERGEN, N., 1953: *Social Behaviour in Animals* (Science Paperbacks edn., 1965).

TINBERGEN, N., 1957: Preface to Schiller (ed.), *Instinctive Behaviour* (New York, International Universities Press).

TINBERGEN, N., 1963: 'On aims and methods of ethology', *Zeitschrift für Tierpsychologie*, 20, 410–33.

TINBERGEN, N., 1966: review of Lorenz's *On Aggression*, *The Listener*, Nov. 17th.

BIBLIOGRAPHY   171

TINBERGEN, N., 1968: 'On war and peace in animals and man', (Inaugural Lecture), published in *Science*, 160, 3835 (June 18th), 1411–18.

TINBERGEN, N. *et al.*, 1962: 'Egg shell removal by the Black-Headed Gull, *Larus ridibundus L.*: A behaviour component of camouflage', *Behaviour*, 19, 74–118.

TROTTER, W., 1916: *Instincts of the Herd in Peace and War* (London, Unwin).

TURNER, V. W., 1966: 'Anthropological Epilogue' to Huxley, (ed.), *Ritualization of Behaviour in Animals and Man*, 521–2.

UCHENDU, V. C., 1964: ' "Kola Hospitality" and Igbo lineage structure', *Man*, Liv., 47–50.

VAN HOOFF, J. A. R. A. M., 1967: 'The facial displays of the Catarrhine monkeys and apes', in Morris (ed.), *Primate Ethology* (London, Weidenfeld & Nicolson), 7–68.

VON-FÜRER-HAIMENDORF, CHRISTOPH, 1967: *Morals and Merit* (London, Weidenfeld & Nicolson).

WARDEN, C. J., 1927: 'The historical development of comparative psychology', *Psychological Review*, 34, 57–85 and 135–68.

WICKLER, WOLFGANG, 1967: 'Socio-sexual signals and their intra-specific imitation among primates', in Morris, (ed.), *Primate Ethology*, 69–147.

WIENER, NORBERT, 1948: *Cybernetics* (New York, Wiley).

WILSON, MONICA, 1951: *Good Company: A Study of Nayakyusa Age-Villages* (London, International African Institute).

WILSON, MONICA, 1960: 'Homicide and Suicide among the Joluo of Kenya', in Bohannan (ed.), *African Homicide and Suicide* (Princeton University Press), 179–213.

WOLFF, KURT H., 1964: 'definition of social control', in Gould and Kolb (eds.), *Dictionary of the Social Sciences*, 650–2.

WYNNE-EDWARDS, V. C., 1962: *Animal Dispersion in Relation to Social Behaviour*, (Edinburgh, Oliver & Boyd).

INDEX